W9-CLG-791

Iraq and the continuing Middle East crisis

Iraq and the continuing Middle East crisis

Ewan W. Anderson
and
Khalil H. Rashidian

Department of Geography
University of Durham

St. Martin's Press
New York

First published in the United States of America in 1991

Printed in Great Britain

ISBN 0-312-05804-7

Library of Congress Cataloging-in-Publication Data

Anderson. Ewan W.
    Iraq and the continuing Middle East crisis / Ewan W. Anderson and
Khalil H. Rashidian.
        p. cm.
    Includes index.
    ISBN 0-312-05804-7
    1. Middle East--Politics and government--1945- I. Rashidian, Khalil H. II. Title.
DS63.1.A54 1991   91-9242
956.04--dc20   CIP

... And soon all of us will sleep under the earth, we
Who never let each other sleep above it.

M. Tsvekayeva (1892–1914)

To our families and the hope of peace and friendship
between East and West.

Contents

List of Figures

List of Tables

Chapter 1
Introduction

The upper Gulf region has, since at least the middle of this century, been considered the major world geopolitical flashpoint. It is at the crossroads of three continents and is the source of more than half of the reserves of the world's most important commodity, oil. Within the vicinity, three of the world's great religions (Judaism, Christianity and Islam) have arisen and there are three, frequently inimical, ethno-linguistic cores: the Jews, the Arabs and the Persians. Into this region, during recent history, have come three major colonial powers: the Turks, the British and the French. Their influence has been at least partly superseded by that of, firstly, the two world superpowers, the United States and the Soviet Union, and, latterly, by the one world 'policeman', the United States. Thus, the potential for misunderstanding and conflict is immense, but three factors are outstanding: nationalism, Islamic fundamentalism and oil.

In the quest for freedom from foreign domination, the ideas of Islam and the Arab nation have frequently taken a strong hold on the imagination of the people. Under President Nasser of Egypt, who successfully opposed the British, the French and, to an extent, the Israelis, the Arabs regained their self-respect. Despite the vast disparities between the various Arab countries in terms of population and, particularly, wealth, common language and culture provide a potent binding force. This bond may have been exaggerated by Arab writers, but it has produced strong anti-colonialist sentiments.

Islamic fundamentalism is not new, but under the Ayatollah Khomeini it achieved new status. It proved immensely appealing to the downtrodden masses of the Middle East and in its name many revolutionary movements have been spawned. Indeed, so potentially potent is its force that Western powers may well have used fundamentalism as a curtain to contain the Soviet Union. Such religious fervour is extremely difficult to contain since it relies upon the spiritual dimension. Against such opposition, worldly arguments are likely to make little headway.

Oil is the driving force of the world economy and the present predominance of the Middle East, and particularly the upper Gulf region, will become even more pronounced by the beginning of the next century.

The major oil consumers and the major producers are separated geographically and it is this which has given rise to the range of geopolitical vulnerabilities. That the main producers are located in the most volatile region of the world exacerbates an already potentially fraught situation.

In this book, these three key elements are examined in detail before an overall threat analysis of the region is made. The Iraq–Kuwait crisis is but one event which has arisen as a result of the complexity of opposing forces in the Middle East. Other such crises will occur and will not be successfully defused until a fuller understanding of the wide variety of factors is achieved and a dialogue is established with the people of the region.

Chapter 2
Colonialism and liberation movements in the Middle East

Colonialism: the background

After the French Revolution in 1789, the idea of the nation-state was taken up enthusiastically throughout Europe. Nationalism and the sense of nationhood became evident.

Europeans with this philosophy aimed to establish their domination outside Europe. By this time, the Ottoman Empire had begun to decline (Figure 2.1) and Turkish troops had lost most of the territory that they had conquered in Europe. A competition began among the major European powers to take over from the Ottomans in the Middle East and North Africa. In France, Napoleon came to power and set out on his Egyptian expedition and entered Palestine. England, after defeating Napoleon, reinforced its influence in the Mediterranean and gained a foothold in the Middle East towards the end of the nineteenth century. France, already a colonial power in North Africa also attempted to extend its influence to the Middle East. The other European powers also tried to establish their own lines of influence in the Middle East, and took every opportunity to intervene and fulfil their ambitions.

From the end of the nineteenth century until the beginning of the First World War, the whole Middle East became the subject of interest of the European Powers. However, they could not reach any agreement. Great Britain was particularly interested in Palestine, France was already influential in Lebanon, and Russia encouraged Russian Jews to emigrate to Palestine as a means of increasing its influence there.[1] Great Britain at the same time supported the Zionist movement in Europe.

In 1914, the Ottoman Turks entered the war on the German side and so the British had to defeat the Turks before they could gain control of the Ottoman

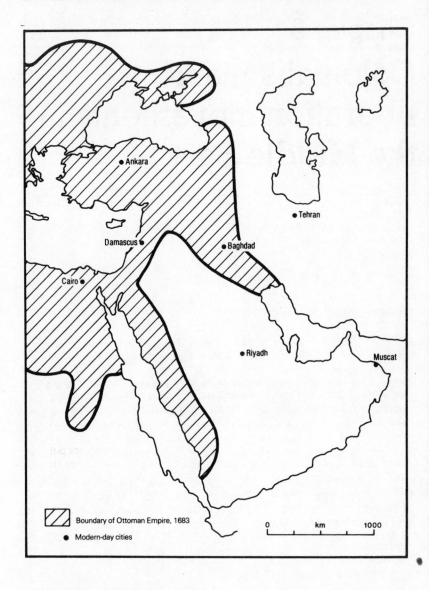

Figure 2.1 The Ottoman Empire, 1683

territories. In the meantime, the Arab nationalists who wanted to be liberated from their Turkish rulers were a potential ally to the British forces in the region. This desire for independence allowed the British to persuade the Arabs to join the European allies against the Axis Powers. It was a choice between remaining loyal to the Islamic state of the Ottoman Empire or taking the opportunity of creating an independent Arab nation through an alliance with the infidel allied forces.

The choice was made basically by the Hashemite Sharif Hussain of Mecca and with this decision the Arabs put their nationalist aspirations ahead of their religious loyalty. Sharif Hussain declared his willingness to support the British troops against the Ottoman Turks. At the same time, the nationalist Arab leaders sent the so-called Damascus Protocol document to Hussain. It contained the conditions that Hussain was to make in return for his support for the British. The main condition was a commitment by the British to grant the Turkish-occupied areas, including Lebanon, the Hejaz, Syria, Iraq, Jordan and Palestine, independence at the end of the war. Furthermore a guarantee was required that the allies would respect the British promise after the war. McMahon, the British High Commissioner in Egypt, accepted the first condition for independence with the exception of the areas of Messina and Alexandretta and parts of Syria west of the towns of Damascus, Homs, Hama and Aleppo.[2] Clearly the excluded areas were Lebanon, the French sphere of influence. In the event Arab support enabled the British troops to cross the Suez Canal and occupy the Sinai. The Arabs thereby played an important part in the victory over the Ottoman Turks.

Before the war ended, regardless of its promise to the Arabs, Great Britain, together with France and Russia, made a secret arrangement to divide the Middle Eastern Arab region into various spheres of influence. According to the Sykes–Picot Agreement (Figure 2.2), France reserved for itself part of Turkey, West Syria and Lebanon, and Great Britain, the southern part of Iraq. Palestine to the west of Jordan was to have an international status under joint British, French and Russian control (with the exception of the harbours of Acre and Haifa, which were to come under British control). As mentioned, Russia encouraged Russian Jews to emigrate to Palestine and with this policy hoped that the Jewish state would become part of their zone of influence.

After the Russian Revolution of 1917, the Bolshevik government published the Agreement, and the Turks took this opportunity to persuade the Arab nationalists to cease their support for Great Britain and the allies. There was also considerable unrest and anger among the Arabs, particularly when they realized that in the Balfour Declaration Great Britain had made a commitment to meet the Zionist demand for Jewish statehood in Palestine.

As a result, Great Britain set about overcoming the problems and embarrassment caused by the revelation of the Sykes–Picot Agreement and the Balfour Declaration.

A new arrangement was initiated by British diplomacy in the region to defuse anti-British and anti-French feeling among the Arab nationalists. In June 1918 a new declaration was made by the British Commissioner in Egypt to the Arab nationalist spokesmen promising that the free elections for Arab governments would be assisted by both Great Britain and France. This declaration was interpreted by the Arabs to mean that the Sykes–Picot Agreement and Balfour Declaration were to be annulled, and Jewish immigrants would be restricted. Up to this point Great Britain had managed

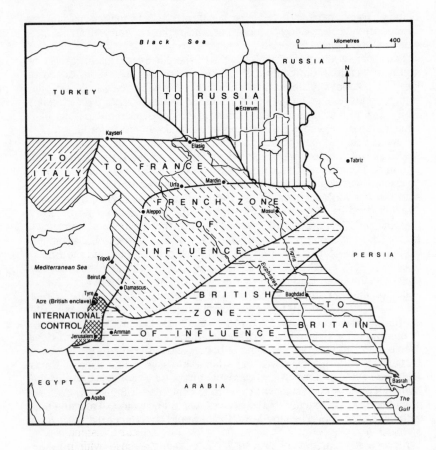

Figure 2.2 The boundaries according to the Sykes–Picot Agreement

to defuse Arab anxiety and in the meantime to secure its superiority in the region by reducing the French zone of influence to Syria and Lebanon.

In July 1919, the General Syrian Congress, an assembly of national leaders from the entire Arab region, called for the complete independence of Greater Syria, which included Palestine, and rejected the European mandate. This revolutionary decision was rejected by France who insisted on a mandate for Syria and Lebanon. France had Great Britain's full support for this demand. All promises and agreements made by Great Britain and France were simply ignored and the nationalist hopes for independence after the war faded.

In 1920, in Sèvres, a peace treaty was signed between the allies and Turkey. The agreement brought Mesopotamia (Iraq), Palestine and Trans Jordan under the British mandate system, and Syria and Lebanon under the French. The Hejaz was the only Arab territory which remained outside the mandate and became independent. The Arabs reacted strongly against the British, French and Zionist plans and decisions. The United States then became involved and played an important role as mediator between the Arabs and Great Britain and France. US President Woodrow Wilson sent a commission to the Middle East to investigate and study the disagreement. The Commission concluded in its report concerning Palestine:

> 'If that principle is to obtain and the wishes of Palestine's population are to be decisive as to what is to be done with Palestine, then it is to be remembered that the non-Jewish population of Palestine, nearly nine-tenths of the whole, are emphatically against the entire Zionist programme. Surveys have shown that there was not one thing upon which the population of Palestine were more agreed than upon this. To subject a people so minded to unlimited Jewish immigration, and to steady financial and social pressure to surrender the land, would be a gross violation of the principle just quoted, and of the peoples rights, though it kept within the forms of Law.'[3]

Finally, the Commission pointed out that the people of Syria were almost unanimous in this view and that, according to British officials, the Zionist programme could only be carried out by force of arms. The report clearly reflected the Arabs' refusal of the mandate and Zionist plans for settlement in Palestine. The Arab desire for independence was also emphasized in the Commission's report.

The British and French mandate (1920–48)

When Great Britain and France conquered and occupied the Ottoman territories in the Middle East, they set up a military administration which later was replaced by civil administrations to rule the areas under their influence.

By the end of the war, both the British and the French had an established force in the region. When the League of Nations granted Great Britain and France the mandate for Palestine and Syria, it emphasized that mandatory powers should only rule indirectly. This was the case with mandate governments in most Arab states except in Palestine, in which Great Britain ruled directly and the mandate government had full legislative, administrative and judicial competence.[4] Britain had also committed itself to call for the founding of a Jewish national home[5] and supported Jewish immigration and settlement. The Arab majority, therefore, demonstrated their resistance and opposition to the mandate in every possible way. This conflict worsened steadily until the end of the mandate. During this period France suppressed the nationalist movement in Damascus which had chosen Feisal as King of the independent Arab state promised by Great Britain. In Iraq there had been several revolts and uprisings and in Jerusalem tension between Arabs and Jewish immigrants increased. The Arab rebellion almost succeeded in the summer of 1938 when many cities, including Jerusalem and much of the countryside fell to the rebels. However, the revolt was crushed in 1939 by British and Zionist forces with a ten-to-one advantage over the Palestinians. The defeat took a high toll on the Palestinian economy, social fabric, and military and political structures. Over 3000

Palestinian people were killed, 110 were hanged, 6000 were placed under detention and 6000–8000 were injured, out of a population of less than a million.[6] This conflict led to the creation of the most painful crisis in the Middle East, which has lasted until the present day.

During 1945 and 1946, immediately after the Second World War ended, the Arab states and the Palestinians made great diplomatic efforts to bring about independence for Palestine and to prevent the partition of Palestine proposed by Britain. After a series of diplomatic and military activities in 1947, the British handed over the Palestine mandate and the responsibility for solving the Arab–Jewish conflict to the United Nations. In May 1947, the United Nations set up a UN Special Committee to deal with the Palestine problem. After a six-month study, the Committee recommended the partition of Palestine into two independent states, with special status for Jerusalem. The Arabs rejected the plan of partition and responded to this proposal by organizing demonstrations and strikes, arguing that in the partition plan the will and consent of the majority Arab nation in Palestine had been ignored. Despite all the Arab efforts, the foundations of the state of Israel were laid down immediately after the British mandatory period was over on 14 May 1948. On 15 May, the provisional Jewish government proclaimed the State of Israel in the heart of the Muslim world, in Palestine.

Revolutionary movements in the Arab world

Twentieth-century revolutionary thought in the Arab world has developed around three ideologies: nationalism, socialism and Islamic fundamentalism.

Nationalism

Nationalist sentiments in the Middle East emerged largely as a result of expansion of European colonialism and Western cultural influences during the nineteenth century. These created new conditions and promoted the rise of a nationalist ideology based on ethno-linguistic identity. This emerged, therefore, as a reaction to foreign cultural and political domination, and particularly to the creation of the British and French mandate systems after the First World War.

During the Ottoman Empire, the development of national identity was a great desire for every non-Turkish nation in the empire. The idea of nationalism developed primarily among the Arab students from Egypt, Palestine, Iraq and Syria, who were trained in the secular military and scientific academies in Istanbul to enforce the Sultan's authority in their bases. Centralization and Turkification strategies adopted by the Ottomans inspired anti-Turkish feeling and strengthened resistance among the nationalist intellectuals.

The collapse of the Ottoman Empire in the aftermath of the First World War did not fulfil nationalist aspirations, and the results of nationalist cooperation with the allies were far below their expectations. Not only were former Ottoman territories divided into several smaller political units under the British and French hegemony, but also Great Britain pledged to support the establishment of Jewish statehood in Palestine.

As the hope for independence and national identity faded so, as a reaction, nationalist activists became more organized and determined to continue their struggle for liberation. As a result of the growing number of intellectuals and educated people within the territories controlled by the British and French, and their communication of shared views, public feeling against foreign domination became an important ideology in the Middle East. At this stage, since there was not a single sovereign Arab state, nationalist ideology was based mainly on the common elements of the Arabic language and the Islamic religion. In the cases of non-Arab nations like the Kurds and Armenians, they developed the sense of nationalism on the basis of their own cultures. The struggle against Western colonialism has never been entirely free from religious sentiment. This was probably because of Christian missionary activities, which led the Muslims to identify the West with Christianity. This attitude led to a political movement that drew its inspiration not only from a desire for freedom and independence, but also from Islam as a religion and for its cultural coherence.

However, the major concern of the Arab nationalists, intellectuals and political activists was to restore sovereignty to the Arab peoples by liberating Arab states from foreign dominance, by the establishment of Western-style parliamentary systems and by the installation of governments independent of traditional religious influences. Indeed, the abolition of the Caliphate by Kamal Ataturk, the Turkish nationalist, intensified the secular tendency among nationalists. Once this prime goal had been achieved the other concern was to secure the coherence of newly established national statehood. In that new sense of nation, the loyalty of political activists was to the national community rather than to the Islamic constitution.

Under the 1920 mandate, Britain installed monarchies in Iraq and Trans Jordan and administered Palestine directly while France governed Syria and Lebanon. During the mandate period, all attempts at liberation were suppressed by British or French forces. When these forces withdrew from the region the result was the division of independent states and conflict which has since created the greatest political turbulence in the region.

Since the creation of Arab nation-states, there have been attempts to combine them using the emotional appeal of nationalism, but few of those attempts have had significant success. Plans for Arab brotherhood and cooperation may survive, but unification of the cultural Arab national into a single political state remains an elusive dream. Representative of this trend is the way in which Egypt has turned away from Pan-Arab concerns towards its own internal affairs and new affirmation of its own regional ties and symbols.[7]

Socialism

After the Second World War, a young generation of Arabs emerged who advocated a more radical view of nationalism, one that would bring about a revolutionary transformation of traditional society.

This new revolutionary ideology has been interpreted as a socialism which was clearly committed to modernization and involved an acceptance of secularism. Although the nationalist leaders in many areas supported programmes of reform and modernization, their main concern was liberation and national unity rather than economic and social improvement. In contrast, socialists attempted to revolutionalize all aspects of public life, with the focus on economic development and the welfare of society which they sought to improve by centralizing all economic policies and power in the state. They achieved this goal through legislation, allowing the nationalization and appropriation of private wealth as well as natural resources and the means of production. They therefore aimed to eliminate control of the economic power of the middle classes, who prospered under nationalist governments.

By the 1960s the dominant ideological position was that of modernizing reformism and in many countries there was a transition from nationalist Westernizers to modernizing nationalist–socialists. This modernizing reformism was largely secular.[8]

Some of the basic characteristics of the new viewpoints included a more clearly materialist perspective, often Marxist in approach, and a willingness to reject even an emotional role for the traditional faith of Islam. There were also efforts to create organizations that would be better integrated and more effective than the personal factions and diffuse schools of thought of the old nationalists and liberals. There was also a more conscious attempt to deal with socio-economic problems. The emphasis of the liberal position had been on individual freedom, especially in intellectual matters, and the winning of political independence.[9]

The early socialist and communist parties and organizations in the Arab countries of the Middle East were often led by people from non-Muslim and minority groups, and such organizations had to bridge the gap between themselves and the majority of the Muslim population if they were to have success. This is illustrated by the experience of the Communist Party in Syria. There, Khalid Bakdash, a communist of Kurdish origin, revitalized the party, and when Soviet policy favoured Arab nationalist causes, as in the mid-1930s, and again in the 1950s, Bakdash and his party prospered.[10]

However, the emergence of Arab socialists to positions of political power in the Arab countries was associated with the new phase of political development, in which the ruling groups that had achieved independence were replaced by a new generation of revolutionary groups. In Syria, the revolution began in 1949 with a series of military coups and reached a climax in 1958 when a union between Syria and Egypt was created by Arab socialist leaders in both countries.

The rejection of the old regime in Egypt came with the revolution in 1952. At that time, the monarchy and the old liberal nationalist parties were all removed by a military coup that brought to power a group of young officers led by Gamal Abd al-Nasser. In Iraq, the monarchy created by the British was overthrown in 1958 by Abd-al Karim Qassem.

The oldest of these movements is the Socialist Arab Ba'ath Party, organized in Syria during the Second World War. It was created by a group of socialist intellectuals led by Michel Aflaq and Salahal Din Baytar. Both men were born in Damascus and received some education in France where they came into contact with the Communist Party. In 1943, the two organized the Ba'ath Party on the basis of a socialist programme of internal reform and a unity programme for all Arabs. Very soon branches of the party were established in Jordan (1948), Lebanon (1949), and Iraq (1950), and an attempt was made to maintain a unified leadership although the party has been plagued by factionalism throughout its history.[11]

The main principles of the Ba'ath ideology were the provision to all Arab nations of equal opportunities to fulful their Arabic national identities and the elimination of traditional elements and artificial classes.

Although the Ba'ath failed in their efforts for Arab unity, they succeeded in becoming a growing force in Syrian politics during the 1950s. Between 1954 and 1958, there was a period of cooperation between the Ba'ath Party and the Communist Party, in which military rule was replaced by a civilian parliamentary system. It was the Ba'ath initiative that persuaded Nasser, the leader of the Egyptian Revolution, to join with Syria in the United Arab Republic (UAR) in 1958. This unity did not last for more than three years and in 1961 Syria became independent again. The relationship between the Ba'ath Party and the Communist Party became very tense and wary and in 1963 the military wing of the Ba'ath Party took control of Syria. At the same time, another military branch of Ba'ath gained control of Iraq. The power struggle among the Ba'athist rivals resulted in another coup in 1966, in which a group of more radical members took power. Both the leaders and founders of the Party, Aflaq and Baytar, went into exile. A similar process occurred in Iraq in 1968. The new generation of the Ba'ath leadership was more pragmatic and proposed programmes for a state-controlled economy and land reform that were more radical than those of Aflaq and Baytar. The new leadership's principles were a combination of radical socialism and nationalism. Their major concern was Arab unity, the need for social and economic reforms, and opposition to imperialist intervention and control both in state and ideology.

The second major Arab nationalist–socialist movement was that in Egypt led by Nasser. The 1952 revolution brought Nasser and a group of young revolutionary officers to power. The basic principles of Nasserism were Arab unity, independence from foreign control, and reform of the traditional style of life and economy. There were great similarities between Nasserist ideology and principles and those of Aflaq and Baytar. The major difference was that Nasserism revolved around Nasser's leadership and personal charisma and Aflaq and Baytar emphasized a collective leadership. Muhammad Haykal, one of the influential journalists and a close adviser to Nasser, described the Nasserism phenomenon as 'The direction of Liberation, social transformation, the people's control of their own resources, and the democracy of the people's working forces'.[12] Both Nasser and Aflaq wished to free the Arab world of foreign control — both wanted to follow a policy of non-alignment on the external scene and both believed that social justice could be achieved only by revolutionary means. However, in 1955–6,

Nasser emerged as the most successful anti-imperialist leader in the Arab world and became the most famous representative of Arab nationalism. The elimination of social and economic injustice was his immediate goal. Through its political achievements internationally and its internal progress, Arab socialism, as an Arabic ideology, became widely accepted among the Arab nations as a popular mass-sentiment. Although Nasser himself was a devout, practising Muslim, he encouraged the socialist ideologies to form a bridge between nationalism and socialism. In the meantime he studied Islamic tenets which might allow him to legitimize his socialist projects. He rejected the secular ideas of communism as an alien and foreign intervention and opposed to the Islamic heritage. Nasser believed that Islamic ideology had potential for the development of an independent socialist ideology. However, the great prestige of Nasser as a revolutionary nationalist and as the leading spokesman for the Arab cause helped to popularize the idea of Islam as being associated with Arab socialism. [13]

By the mid-1960s, Arab socialism in various forms appeared to be the most popular ideology among the intellectuals in the Middle East. Nasserism and the Ba'ath were the two leading exponents of that view, but there were many political activities and movements based on similar principles in other areas in the Middle East. Arab nationalist–socialist regimes — already established in Syria, Egypt and Iraq — became models of ideal governments for the political activists to achieve. In 1962, a military group overthrew the Yemeni regime and espoused those ideas. In Lebanon, Jordan and many conservative Arab states there were also active movements of that persuasion. The Palestine national movement expressed itself basically in Arab socialist terms.

However, by the end of 1960 the picture was clearly changing and internal divisions and reorientations of socialist thought and practice were preparing the way for the new mood of the 1970s onwards. This period saw the rise of oil-producing power, Arab solidarity, and Islamic militant tendency in the Muslim world.

Egypt and Syria were no longer regarded as influential and Arab cultural and political centres of gravity. In fact the Arab focus was moved from the traditional sites in the north to the Persian Gulf and Arabian Peninsula in the south of the Arab world. This was particularly influenced by the Six-Day War between Arabs and Israel in 1967 which undermined the radical leadership of Nasser in Egypt and the Ba'ath regime in Syria, both of which represented the mainstream of revolutionary Arab politics. Eventually Egypt and Syria became partially dependent upon the oil-producing countries in the Persian Gulf area.

The death of Nasser in 1970 left a leadership vacuum in the Arab world resulting in rivalry between Iraq, Syria and Saudi Arabia for leadership of the Arab nation.

The Palestine question

Historical background

Since Biblical times, Arabs and Jews have been living together in peace and respect, and throughout the history of Islam, there have always been close relationships between Muslims and Jews. Both Jews and Christians were under their own spiritual heads even in civil and criminal judicial procedures, and were not forced to have Muslim law applied to them — a system which lasted until the Ottoman and mandate periods. For centuries, Muslims and Jews lived together in harmony, a harmony which was disturbed when the Zionists began to claim that Palestine was the rightful possession of the Jewish people alone.

The first signs of hostility between the Arabs and the Jews appeared when a riot broke out in Jerusalem in protest against mass Jewish immigration to Palestine. This event was followed by British commitment to the creation of a Jewish homeland in Palestine. For more than sixty years four generations of Palestinians have suffered as refugees. They have spread throughout the region and indeed around the world, while some have been kept in semi-military camps in occupied Palestine. Four generations of continuous struggle have been directed towards a return to their homeland and the establishment of a free and independent state. The study of the Palestinian problem is not only of importance in understanding Palestinian aspirations for a national state; it also illuminates one of the fundamental elements of the Middle East crisis. To understand the Palestinian phenomenon, it is necessary to review briefly the social and political environment in which it has developed.

The main factors which influenced the modes of political action of the Palestinians at the end of the Ottoman period and during the early part of the British mandate, were the increasing public awareness and politicization. These resulted from Western cultural influences in the form of the parliamentary system and the voluntary organization of people with common interests or political conceptions. Organizations for the advancement of Arab cultural and political interests developed national associations whose programmes evolved from demands for administrative reform to the idea of national separatism.

Towards the end of the First World War when the Balfour Declaration was issued (1917), a drastic shift in the theme and direction of political activity became apparent in Palestine. The British motivation behind the Balfour Declaration was a mixture of self-interest and an acute desire to do good for the Jews. Furthermore there was the additional temptation for Great Britain to secure a foothold along the eastern approaches to the Suez Canal. The revelation of British–French and Zionist plans led to the acceleration of a process which, under normal circumstances, would have developed more gradually.

British support for the arrival of Jewish immigrants in large numbers exacerbated the hostility between Arabs and Jews. The Palestinian Arabs saw Zionism as a political movement enjoying the protection and support of

Great Britain and France but threatening their political, economic and social structure. The organizations of nationalists, Islamic traditionalists and socialists began to form to combat the Zionists in Palestine. Palestinian organizations were obliged to adopt a position regarding not only Zionism, but also the country's political future.

In order to ease the anxiety of the Arabs, the British and French published their famous declaration of November 1918. This declared the rights of Syrians and Iraqis to establish governments deriving their authority from the popular will. Despite raising some hope, Arab reaction was neither optimistic nor positive. They argued that the independence of states is a natural right and should not be used to compensate for other undemocratic decisions. The Palestinian argument was simple: the Arabs were not responsible for the oppression of the Jews in Europe. Besides, Palestine, with its limited resources, could not cope with large-scale Jewish immigration. Finally, the creation of a Jewish state in Palestine would certainly eradicate its Arab national and cultural identity.

These arguments, protests and political activities did not deter Britain from its commitment to the establishment of a Jewish state and the steady flow of Jewish immigrants into Palestine resulted in the Arab–Jewish riots of 1921 and 1929.[14]

During the 1920s the Zionists in Palestine had formed an underground military organization called Haganah, and an extremist offshoot of this body named the Irgun was responsible for major Jewish terrorist activities in Palestine. Yet another group, the Stern Gang, devoted itself exclusively to political violence.

The Arab answer to organized Zionist violence was the establishment of the Arab Higher Committee headed by Mufti Jamal al-Hussayni which united all Arab political groups and activists into a common front. To coordinate Arab resistance, national committees were formed in most towns and villages in Palestine. Hussayni exercised his religious and political leadership through the executive committee and the newly established Supreme Muslim Council.[15] As it became clear that the British forces would not leave Palestine and other mandate territories, the activities of the Arabs and Palestinian political organizations against both British and Zionists increased but without major achievements. From 1936 to 1939 groups of young Muslims began to organize themselves on an exclusively religious basis, both within the young men's Muslims' Associations and the youth scouting associations. These played a significant role against the British and the Zionists.

Another faction which became an important factor in the Arab communities particularly in Palestine were the university graduates, whose familiarity with the English and French languages and Western culture made them natural spokesmen. The rise of this new action in the region coincided with a move towards independence in the Fertile Crescent and the consequent development of an ideological basis for Arab unity. As the Arab countries approached self-rule, they began to question its implications, and a process of ideologizing of the Arab national movement took place. The doctrine of Arab unity was preached by the great Arab nationalist, Sati al-

Husri, and his colleagues. This trend influenced many educated people in Palestine and provided the first basis for the ideological organization, the Istiqlal (Independent) Party which, while theoretically and ideologically a branch of a Pan-Arab organization, was in practice a local Palestinian party. It was intended to be a Pan-Arab movement, much like the Ba'ath Party in the 1950s. The importance of the Istiqlal Party was its struggle against Zionism as an element in the wider issue of Arab independence and unity.[16] The Istiqlal remained a source for the flow of educated youth into the Husayni camp, so that the overwhelming majority of the educated Palestinian generation of the 1930s joined the Husayni camp and accepted the leadership of Hajj Amin. The force that Husayni and his supporters had built up remained and even increased in the 1940s. Under the Husayni leadership a radical policy was adopted towards the British administration and also towards Jewish extremists.

Another important organization which developed in the 1940s in Palestine was the Arab Communist Party, the League of National Liberation. It was in fact the left wing of the national movement and emphasis was placed on social reform.

Despite some measure of achievement in the establishment of self-ruling regimes in Iraq, Hejaz (Saudi Arabia) and Jordan, all efforts made by the various factions and organizations to liberate the Arab states in the Middle East were unsuccessful. The Palestine question remained unsolved and all hope for a peaceful settlement faded.

The establishment of the Jewish statehood of Israel in Palestine triggered a new stage of conflict between Arab Muslims and the Jews, which involved the Jewish communities worldwide and Islamic communities in the region.

Palestine and the United Nations

The Palestine drama began to move rapidly towards its tragic destiny immediately after the 1948 war started between Arab states and Israel. Before the war, a UN Special Committee appointed to examine the issue in its entirety, submitted two reports in September 1947. The reports recommended that Palestine should be constituted in the form of an independent Arab state and an independent Jewish state with a High Commissioner with direct control of the areas around Jerusalem and Bethlehem together with the Negev. Seven of the eleven committee members came out in favour of a so-called majority plan which envisaged the partition of Palestine, and a minority of three preferred a state with a federal structure, with a Jewish and an Arab region and Jerusalem as the capital. The Zionists accepted the majority plan. The Arab Higher Committee called it 'absurd', impracticable and unjust, besides being incompatible with the principles of self-determination enshrined in the UN Charter. The Arabs proposed that the matter should be decided by the International Court of Justice at the Hague.

Despite Arab opposition, the Partition Plan, recommended by the majority, was adopted by a two-thirds majority of the General Assembly on 29 November 1947. Then it had to be implemented. The geographical realities of Palestine together with the political and demographic structure of its population constituted the first difficulty. The United Nations attempted to persuade Great Britain as the major force in the region to guarantee the implementation of the plan. Great Britain was, however, reluctant to take on this responsibility and refused to cooperate in any plan that might involve further violence. Indeed it soon announced that it would withdraw its troops from Palestine, which it did on 15 May 1948. Thus the United Nations had no military power to implement the resolution in Palestine. Meanwhile the Zionists had already begun to force through the Partition Plan by violence.

In Palestine, the Arab High Committee called a general strike in December 1947 and boycotted the Jews in Palestine. The Arab states declared that they would use military force to support the Palestinians in their resistance to the Partition Plan, but they decided not to act while the British troops were still present in Palestine. As soon as the British withdrew the Jews seized most of the important towns and rural areas. The Jewish agencies Irgun, Stern and Haganah created an atmosphere of terror among the Arab Palestinians. The brutal massacre of a hundred Arab women and children in Dayryasin sparked the exodus of about 200,000 Arabs from their homes. Finally, a few hours before the termination of the mandate the Jewish National Council proclaimed on 14 May 1948 the establishment of the State of Israel.

The total population of Palestine in 1948 was estimated to be 2,115,000, of which 1,380,000 were Arab Muslims and Christians, and one-third, 700,000, were Jews. Jewish land ownership in the whole of Palestine rose from 0.5 per cent in 1918 to about 6 per cent in 1948. Under the Partition Plan, the Jewish state was to comprise 56 per cent (5893 square miles) of the total area of Palestine: the Arab state was to be 43 per cent (4475 square miles); and the international zone of Jerusalem and surrounding areas, less than 1 per cent (68 square miles). Jewish land holdings in the proposed area of the Jewish state were less than 10 per cent (345,964 acres out of a total land area of 3,690,000 acres) but the population was to be half Arab and half Jewish.[17]

The state of Israel (1948) and the first Arab–Israeli war

The creation of Israel immediately led to armed confrontation between the new-born state of Israel and the neighbouring Arab countries which promptly attacked it. The armed struggles between militant Jewish agencies and the Palestinian resistance movement started even before the UN Partition Plan. However, the Arab Legion arrived in Palestine in answer to urgent appeals from the Palestine Arabs who were being subjected to Zionist atrocities, expulsion and dispossession. The Arab forces consisted of units from Trans Jordan, Syria, Lebanon, Iraq and Egypt, but what eventually gave the Israelis the upper hand on the battlefield was:

(a) superiority in numbers, arms, training and organization;
(b) resourcefulness and unity of purpose;
(c) confidence, determination and high morale.

The Arabs, on the other hand, did not have a joint command and lacked coordinated field action. They also did not agree on the purpose for entering the war. Therefore, their defeat was inevitable. During the various periods of ceasefire in July, Israel was able to make itself strong enough to reach the front lines which later became the demarcation lines after the armistice with neighbouring countries which were agreed in the first half of 1949.

At the end of the first Arab–Israeli war, the new state of Israel controlled 77.4 per cent of Palestine, despite the fact that the UN Partition Plan had allocated only 56.4 per cent for them. (Figure 2.3). In 1949, Jews owned 72.3 per cent of the total area.

This first in a long series of Israeli military successes meant that Israel had not only ignored the UN Partition resolution but had also shown, by refusing to allow Palestinian refugees to return, that it was not prepared to tolerate an Arab–Palestinian state in Palestine. The victory brought Israel more land, but it did not bring peace. On the contrary, it laid the foundations for the confrontation that has continued until the present day.

Israel's desire for expansion

The Partition Plan not only gave the Zionists part of Palestine, it also constituted the official recognition by the United Nations of a sovereign Jewish state, the goal towards which they had been striving since Herzel. This was only a first step in their dream of a greater Israel.

During the Second World War it was Zionist policy to force the Palestinian Arabs to quit their homes. This policy, which had such success, had two distinct advantages: (a) it ensured that no potential danger remained as a fifth column and (b) it changed the balance of Arab–Jew population. It also created a new element in the region — the refugee. The four Armistice Agreements of 1949 provided the Israelis with a new recognized boundary. The return of the refugees to their homeland was opposed and the exodus of Palestinian Arabs continued.

The Israeli rejection of responsibility for the refugees is often sustained by the theory that they were not driven from their homes, but fled of their own free will or at the instigation of their leaders who promised them quick victory. In reality, even the Zionists do not deny the fact that it was all part of their plan for the reconquest of the Promised Land, in which there was no room for large, hostile, alien groups.[18] The Plan was supported by propaganda calculated to impress Western views.

From 1948 to 1956, Israel not only attacked towns and villages directly under its control but also launched military attacks on neighbouring areas. Although Zionist sympathizers in the West tried to justify the Israeli aggression, they could not prevent Israel's condemnation by the United Nations Security Council in 1951, 1953, 1955 and 1956.

Despite all condemnations, however, Israel's attitude towards the Palestinian Arabs remained unchanged. Nahum Goldmann, the President of the Twenty-Sixth World Zionist Congress publicly stated in 1964 that the task of the Zionist movement was 'to make use of the Jewish State as a means of securing the future of the Jewish people throughout the world'.[19] The regime in Israel never showed any great interest in searching for a peace settlement

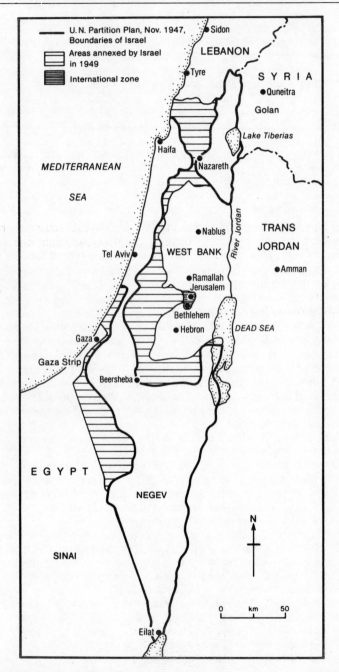

Figure 2.3 The boundaries of Israel

in the region or in solving the Palestinian question. As a result, the conflicts between Israel and Palestine and the Arab states have systematically escalated.

The Palestinian refugees

From spring 1948 to spring 1949, streams of Palestinian Arab refugees left their homeland. They took with them their door keys, but after three generations these have become only a symbol of their determination to return. 'About 900,000 individuals shared this collective fate forgotten by the world, humiliated, insulted, despairing and silent.'[20]

The first refugees were forced to live in fields, while others lived in mosques, churches, monasteries, schools and abandoned buildings. In June 1950, 29.3 per cent of refugees recognized by the UN World Refugees Association (UNWRA) were housed in camps. This estimate rose to 38.6 per cent by June 1957. Since 1956 tents in the fifty-six UNWRA camps have been replaced by emergency accommodation. The refugees' plight was one of poverty but those who received UNWRA aid were better off than the rest. On account of the UNWRA definition of a 'refugee', 48 per cent of Palestinians received nothing at all. It is no exaggeration to say that UNWRA rations were not enough to live on but just too much to die on,[21] and inadequate food supplies inevitably led to disease.

The main refugee camps were set up in Jordan, Lebanon, Syria and the Gaza Strip. The host countries, who were unable to provide jobs for their own people, simply could not cope with thousands of refugees. The refugees themselves were hopeful of returning to their homelands and therefore regarded their situation as temporary. In this context the United Nations passed two resolutions, the first in 1948 and the second in 1953, on the right of the Palestinians either to return home or to receive compensation. Israel refused to recognize these resolutions. The main Israeli concern was the control and security of the Occupied Territories.

Arnold Toynbee[22] considered 'the Jewish treatment of the Arabs in 1947 as morally indefensible as the slaughter by the Nazis of 6,000,000 Jews'. He said 'The most tragic thing in human life is when people who have suffered impose suffering in their turn.'

Since the 1948-9 Arab–Israeli war the number of Palestinian refugees has steadily increased as a result of high birth rates and expulsions from the Occupied Territories. The Palestinian refugees can be categorized into three groups:

(a) those who live in the camps, inside Israel or in the neighbouring Arab states;
(b) those who live in the Arab oil-rich countries in the Persian Gulf region or the countries of North Africa;
(c) those who fled the region and now live mainly in the West, in Europe, the United States and Canada.

Population statistics for the Palestinian refugees vary according to source. It

is reasonable to assume that about four million Palestinians live in the immediate peripheral area or within the homeland as defined by the refugee groups and that over one million live outside the area. Table 2.1 gives an estimate of the total Palestinian population from 1952 to 1987 and Table 2.2 shows the distribution of the Palestinian population registered as refugees in June 1988.

The refugees who live in the camps in Israel or in the Lebanon, Jordan or Syria are in a worse situation compared with those who live outside the region. The camp refugees are prisoners of their faith and fate, frustrated by idleness and an unknown future. They perpetuate the confrontational nature of the political problems involved in the region.

In 1949, the United Nations High Commissions for Refugees (UNHCR) sent the Economic Survey Mission to deal with the problem of Palestinian refugees. In their report the mission recommended the following:

> UNRWA should (1) 'continue with the existing relief programme but provide for a termination of UN relief by 31 December 1950 at the latest,' (2) 'provide a programme of public works until 30 June 1951 as a substitute for the abandoned relief programme,' and (3) 'promote economic development as a basis for permanent settlement.'[23]

The Economic Survey Commission's recommendations were nullified by Israel's refusal to readmit refugees. Israel in fact never agreed to repatriate more than 100,000 refugees and only then as part of a general peace settlement. Indeed, only 4600 refugees have been formally repatriated as part of an Egyptian–Israeli Peace Agreement in 1986.[24]

The hope for a return to the homeland has sustained the Palestinian refugees since 1948 and as a result the camps have existed for more than forty years without significant change in the basic structure of refugee life. Neither UN resolutions nor human rights protests have exerted enough pressure on Israel or its Arab neighbour states to replace the camps with better dwellings. Indeed, the political, social and economic difficulties of the Palestinians in the Arab states were never successfully addressed by UNRWA. There is no doubt that the Palestinian refugees who live in the camps are the main sufferers in the Arab–Israeli conflict. They are more vulnerable to the interplay of power between the Arab states and among the Palestinian political organizations as well.

The Palestinian resistance

As a result of their rejection and humiliation the Palestinians learned new laws of survival: to rely on themselves and take their fate into their own hands and to express themselves through organizations. They sought work throughout the world and they found that education was a guarantee for the future. Groups were formed in the camps and courses started, while for those who lived outside there were better opportunities. A new movement was initiated of directed resistance and struggle. At the time the themes of Arab unity and liberal nationalism were very popular. Nasser in Egypt and Michel Aflaq's Ba'ath Party in Syria and Iraq moved the Arabs towards

Table 2.1 Estimate of total Palestinian population, 1952–1987

	1952		1961		Before June 1967		After June 1967		1982		1987	
Historic Palestine	1,221,300	76.4	1,430,000	64.4	1,668,200	63.4	1,344,868	49.7	1,856,300	41.0	2,140,400	41.6
Israel	179,300	11.2	242,000	10.9	318,200	12.1	325,700	12.0	550,000	12.2	645,000	12.5
West Bank	742,000	48.4	814,000	36.7	900,000	34.2	664,494	24.6	830,000	18.3	937,400	18.2
Gaza	300,000	18.8	374,000	16.8	450,000	17.1	354,674	13.1	476,300	10.5	558,000	10.9
		65.2		53.5		51.3		37.3		28.8		29.1
UNRWA operations	1,389,000	86.9	1,867,400	84.1	2,156,000	82.0	2,117,768	78.3	3,006,300	66.3	3,369,000	65.5
	347,000	21.7	679,400	30.6	806,300	30.7	1,098,600	40.6	1,700,000	37.5	1,873,600	36.5
Jordan	150,000	9.4	380,000	17.1	466,000	17.7	730,600	27.0	1,080,000	23.8	1,282,000	24.4
Syria	83,000	5.2	116,400	5.2	140,300	5.4	143,000	5.3	245,000	5.4	284,000	5.5
Lebanon	114,000	7.1	183,000	8.3	200,000	7.6	225,000	8.3	375,000	8.3	337,600	6.6
Other sources	31,200	1.9	110,000	5.0	155,500	5.9	263,162	9.7	975,000	21.5	1,125,500	21.9
Arab World	—	—	—	—	128,000	4.9	216,162	8.0	800,000	17.6	927,000	18.0
Non-Arab	—	—	—	—	27,500	1.0	47,000	1.7	175,000	3.9	198,000	3.9
Total sources	1,599,500	100.0	2,219,400	100.0	2,630,000	100.0	2,706,630	100.0	4,531,300	100.0	5,139,000	100.0

Source: L. Hajjar, (comp) 'The Palestinian Journey, 1952–1987', *MERIP Middle East Report* Bd. 17, No. 3, S. 10, Washington DC, May–June 1987.

Table 2.2 Distribution of registered Palestinian population, 30 June 1988

Area	Population	Number of camps	Total camp population*	Registered persons not in camps	Percentage of population not in camps
Lebanon	288,176	13	148,007	140,169	48.64
Syria	265,221	10	77,779	187,442	70.67
Jordan	870,490	10	213,539	656,951	75.47
West Bank	385,634	20	100,499	285,153	73.94
Gaza Strip	459,074	8	253,008	206,066	44.89
Total	2,268,595	61	792,832	1,475,763	65.05

*It is estimated that a further 52,000 persons, who are not registered refugees, live in camps. About 37,000 of these are persons displaced as a result of the June 1967 hostilities.
Source: Ashkenasi Abraham, The Jerusalem Journal of International Relations. Vol. 12, No. 1, January 1990.

liberation and unity. The new generation of Palestinians were the potential recruits for this movement.

The Arab nationalists (Al-Qaumiyun-al-Arab), founded and led by the Palestinian George Habbas, and the Palestinian Students' Federation in Cairo, founded and led by Yasser Arafat, Abu Iyyad, Farouk Kaddoumi and by members of the Ba'ath Party, were probably the first organizations to provide the Palestinians with an opportunity to discuss the fate of their people with political movements. To attract sympathy and support of the socialist and liberal groups, Yasser Arafat, as the President of the Students' Federation, made great efforts in travelling and presenting the Palestinian case. At the same time, the Palestinians in the Gaza Strip began to form underground groups. After the occupation of the Gaza Strip by Israel in 1956, the al-Fatah organization, as a common front of all Palestinians, came to the fore to bring all Palestinian resistance groups under one umbrella, regardless of their political differences. This led to the foundation of the National Unity Front, al-Fatah in 1955.[25] The establishment of the al-Fatah organization was regarded as the direct organized Palestinian challenge of Israel. The organization also succeeded in spreading its influence among the Palestinian refugee groups. Soon afterwards al-Fatah decided to take up the armed struggle against Israel. The proclamation of this strategy was opposed by the Ba'athists and other Arab organizations, convinced that only a united Arab army could liberate Palestine. However, al-Fatah defended the strategy strongly and organized the armed struggle. Ironically, the Palestinian representatives were now following in the footsteps of the Zionist movement.

On 1 June 1964, the 1st Palestinian National Council met and founded the Palestine Liberation Organization (PLO). The PLO's official aim was to liberate Palestine and a national fund for donations was set up. The Palestine Liberation Army (PLA) was to be the military arm of the PLO. Ahmad

Shukairy, a diplomat and lawyer, became the first chairman of the PLO Executive Committee. Shukairy must be credited with drafting the Palestinian National Charter and thereby presenting a manifesto which for the first time formulated the idea of a Palestinian identity. Growing pressure for a war of national liberation forced Shukairy to resign on 24 December 1967.

The Fourth Congress of the Palestinian National Council in July 1988 called for freedom of movement for the commandos in the states bordering Israel. It also rejected UN Security Council Resolution 242 in which the Palestinians and their rights were not mentioned. The Palestinians were referred to only indirectly as a 'refugee problem'.

After the Fourth Congress, the PLO set out on a new path: the path of armed struggle and of a separate, independent Palestinian resistance movement.[26]

The uprising (Intifada) in the Occupied Territories

While international attention has been focused on the Iraqi invasion of Kuwait and the explosive situation in the Persian Gulf, the 1.4 million Palestinians residing in the West Bank and Gaza Strip face a steadily deteriorating situation. The Palestinian reaction to the movement of Israeli settlers and to government plans for further expansion has been expressed in a totally new way. The uprising or Intifada involves not the armed Palestinian guerillas but the children, the women and even the elderly. The Israeli response to this new phenomenon of protest has been strong but unsuccessful. This mass protest has brought the dream of an independent homeland closer to reality and its psychological effects on the younger generations are profound.

The views and actions of the Palestinians in these territories are far more important than those everywhere else. They will be a factor in the ultimate success or failure of the attempt to implement a peace programme based on Israeli security and Palestinian self-determination and statehood.

The roots of the Intifada lie in the history of the refugees. In recent years, the Israeli government has consolidated its hold on the West Bank and Gaza by rapid expansion of settlements and suppression of the Palestinian institutions and leadership. The Israelis assume that the West Bank and Gaza are part of the historic land of Israel and that Jews have a God-given right to settle and exercise sovereignty over the land.[27] The number of Jewish settlers living in the territories has increased dramatically from about 3000 in 1977 to more than 80,000 in 1989. With the new waves of Jewish immigrants from the Soviet Union and Eastern Europe, it is expected that the Jewish population in the West Bank will equal that of the Arabs within a few years.

In addition to the settlement programme, the Israeli authorities have vigorously exercised other policies of political control. For example, they have placed severe restrictions on the operation of Arab universities and schools in the West Bank and Gaza. Palestinian universities have also been closed intermittently and sometimes for extended periods. Other measures of control include censoring, closing or limiting the distribution of Arabic newspapers published in East Jerusalem and placing restrictions on travel, sometimes as a form of house or town arrest for individuals or sometimes for whole communities as a form of collective punishment. This intensified and systematic suppression has pushed the Palestinians into a reactionary position which has produced the Intifada.

The Kurds: a nation without a state and without friends

Gerard Chaliand,[28] in *People Without a Country*, wrote:

> Throughout the world the oppression of minorities manifests itself to varying extents and in a wide variety of forms including:
>
> Discrimination: rejection of those who belong to a given group.
> Cultural oppression: deprivation of the minority's right to use its own language in school, in publications and in dealings with the administration.
> Economic oppression: a systematic bias against the interests of the minority.
> Physical oppression: massive implantation of the majority ethnic group or occupation of the minority's territory by means of population transfer.
> Genocide: the attempt to eliminate the minority community as a whole.

The Kurds as a nation artificially divided between several states in the Middle East form minorities which can be categorized according to Chaliand's classification. However, for more than 20 million people with 3000 years of history living in an area of more than 500,000 square kilometres, the term 'minority' may seem inappropriate (Figure 2.4).

The Kurds, who established one of the oldest civilized communities in the world, long before the appearance of the Turks or the Arabs as a nation in the region, are still being denied the right to use their own language and to have an identity of their own.

The Kurds, the fourth-most numerous people in the Middle East, make up probably the largest nation in the world which has been denied an independent state. Whatever the criteria or measures used to define it the Kurds are entitled to a national identity. They are still struggling to protect their national inheritance which they have preserved for centuries. In fact struggle is second nature for the Kurds. It began with the harshness of nature and continued with the ruthlessness of invaders, the Assyrians, the Persians, the Greeks, the Romans, the Arabs, the Mongols and the Turks.

Since the beginning of this century, in which nationalism as an ideology has led to the recognition of national identity, the Kurdish nationalists have laid strong claims for national identity. In the division of the Ottoman Empire after the First World War, the Kurds were offered the prospect of independence under the Treaty of Sèvres (1920) but later this was denied them. For the Kurds the Treaty of Sèvres has remained a crucial reference point for subsequent appeals to the conscience of the world and they continue to claim that by race, language, life style, and most importantly by geography they form a distinct nation. Periodically the Kurds have won sympathy from outside the region but never enough to fulfil their desire for

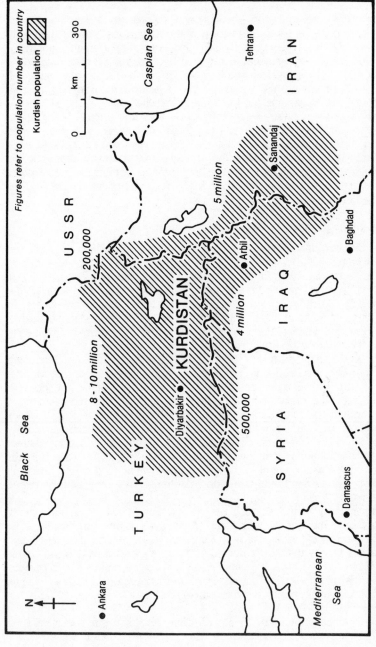

Figure 2.4 The Kurds and Kurdistan

national statehood.

Today the homeland of the Kurdish people, Kurdistan, lies in five different independent states. The vast majority of the Kurdish people still live in the rural areas of this large mountainous region, concentrated mainly in Turkey, Iran and Iraq, with a smaller number in Syria and the Soviet Union. The governments of Turkey, Iran and Iraq, which have had recurrent disputes in their relationships on the various issues, have always agreed on a single issue: cooperation against the Kurds and Kurdish identity.

However, given the strategic location of Kurdistan, the continuing conflicts and the vital issue of national resources (oil, water and unexploited minerals), the Kurdish case retains a high priority for the neighbouring regimes. Time after time when the disagreements between them reach a certain level Kurdistan becomes the battleground for their rivalries. History is constantly being repeated and the Kurds, without a country, have no allies and few prospects for the future.

Who are the Kurds?

The Kurds are descendants of an Indo-European tribe which settled in the region about 4000 years ago. The earliest record refers to the Kurds in Xenophon's *Anabasis*. When 10,000 Greeks retreated from Persia (400 BC), they passed through the Zagros Mountains where they encountered the Karduchoi (Kardu). Minorsky is of the opinion that there is nothing really surprising in the finding at that time of an Iranian tribe settled to the north of the Tigris, 'but we have nothing but the evidence of the name from which to judge the ethnology of the Karduchoi'.[29]

The Kurds as the people of the mountain have had a difficult relationship with those of the surrounding plains. Early on they were in conflict with the Sumer, and with Babylon and Assyria. Despite the cultural and political influences of the Arabs and Turks, the Kurds had developed a distinct and independent national identity, having no ethnic relationship with either Turks or Arabs. On the contrary, Kurdish culture and language are closely related to those of the Persians. The Kurds are regionally divided into dialect groups which cannot communicate freely with other Kurds in their mother tongue. The Kurdish language is composed of two major dialects: Kermanji and Sorani and a number of sub-dialects including Hawramy, Laki, Badinani, Gurani and Garusi.

The majority of the Kurdish people are Sunnite Muslims but a small proportion in Iran and Iraq are Shiite Muslims, Assyrians, and Yasidis.

The majority of the Kurds live in Kurdistan (a geographical expression of the areas where the Kurds live). Kurdistan is marked as a mountainous region stretching from south east Turkey and northern parts of Syria across the northernmost areas of Iraq into Iran's western region. In addition it spills over into Soviet Armenia and Azerbaijan. This area totals some 500,000 sq. km.

Giving an accurate figure for the Kurdish population is not easy because the governments of the Kurdistan region either deny Kurdish existence as a whole or attempt to minimize the Kurdish population. Since the Iranian government has always claimed the Kurds as pure Iranian, no statistics on the national composition of the population have ever been made available. It is clear, however, that the overwhelming majority of the population of Kurdistan in Iran is Kurdish. The figures in Table 2.3 give some idea of its importance.[30]

Table 2.3 The Kurd population in Iran, 1970, 1975

Year	Iran (total)	Kurds in Iran	% of Kurds in the Iranian population
1970	28,258,800	4,803,860	16
1975	32,440,000	5,190,400	16

The same story applies to the government of Iraq which has no statistics about the size of the various ethnic groups or has decided not to make them public. The total population of Kurdistan in Iraq in 1975 was estimated to be 2,800,000.[31]

Kurdistan in Turkey is the largest and most populous part of Kurdish national territory. According to the general census of 1970, the population of Kurdistan in Turkey numbered 8,500,000 Kurdish speakers which represented 23.8 per cent of the population of the Republic of Turkey (total population 35.7 million in 1970).[32]

According to the 1970 general census there were 278,400 people in the Kurdish colonies of Armenia, Azerbaijan, Georgia, Kazakhstan, Kirghisia and Turkoman.[33]

A cautious estimate of the Kurdish population based on the rate of population increase for each state since 1970 is set out in Table 2.4.

Table 2.4 Current estimate of total Kurdish population

Country	No. of Kurds (millions)	% of total population
Iran	5.7	11
Iraq	4.0	23
Turkey	10.2	21
Syria	0.9	8
USSR	0.3	—
Estimated total	21.1	

The Kurdish character and social structure

The Kurdish character has frequently been described by Islamic and European historians, travellers and government officials. In all these assessments, which tend to be romanticized and exaggerated, it is clearly shown that the Kurds differ from the Turks, the Arabs and even the Persians. Environment, life style and social structure are among the factors that characterize certain groups of people. There are additional, very significant features that apply to the Kurdish character.

Physically, the Kurds are generally taller and thinner than Arabs and Turks. Socially, they tend to be loyal, tolerant and independent. Originally, the Kurds were nomads who would spend the winter in the lowland villages and graze their flocks in the highlands in the summer. However, since the sixteenth century the Kurdish nomadic way of life has come under attack from various governments.

Today, not only has nomadism all but disappeared, but feudalism and even landlordism have also declined. Detribalized Kurds have been driven off the land to the major towns and cities where they have become for the most part unskilled labourers, but occasionally trained professionals. Despite some high achievements in the military, politics and other professions, they have usually been discriminated against.[34]

Racially the Kurds are distinct and the Kurdish language distinguishes them from Turkic speakers in Turkey and Semitic-speaking Arabs in Iraq and Syria. Though the Kurdish language and Farsi (Iranian language) are from the same origin, 'Parsi', they are not mutually intelligible. With regard to religion, the majority of Kurds in Iran are of the Sunnite sect. Since the state religion is Shiism, Kurds who might ordinarily live as equal with their racial brothers are alienated on the grounds of religion. Finally, the tribal social structure has enabled the Kurds to preserve many of their ancient traditions.

Modern Kurdish movements and the Iraqi regimes

The modern history of the Kurds dates from the establishment of the Ottoman Empire in the sixteenth century. When the Ottomans sought to resist the rising power of the Shiite Safavids dynasty in Persia, they secured the support of the Kurdish principalities. The Persian armies were defeated and the Kurds remained a turbulent political factor between the two empires. In turn, however, the Kurdish tribes were themselves manipulated into exhausting rivalries which prevented cohesion and the rise of any individual leader capable of uniting them all. There were repeated uprisings against both the Turks and the Persians but the consequences were always disastrous for the Kurds, resulting in mass banishments to remote areas. It was only in the 1880s that there arose Kurdish leaders who had the vision of uniting Kurdish people of both empires into one state.

In Kurdistan at the end of the nineteenth century, there were two general types of charismatic leader: the religious leaders and tribal leaders. The religious category was made up of Sufi Shaikhs. Sufism is a particular approach to practising religion. In Kurdistan the Sufi orders with the largest following were the Qadiri and the Naqshbandi. The former was founded by a famous saint, Shaikh Abdul Qader al-Gailani (1077–1166).[35] Until recent years the path (the way of indoctrination) was highly respected. The Naqshbandi order was founded by Muhammad Baha Ud-Din of Bukhara (1317–89).[36] Both the Qadiri and the Naqshbandi orders are part of the Sunnite sect of Islam.

Among the foremost Sufi leaders in Kurdistan were Shaikh Said and Shaikh Mahmud of Barzinji in Iraq, Shaikh Obaidullah of Shamdinan and

Shaikh Ahmad of Barzan (northern Iraq), and Shaikh Said of Turkey. These leaders struggled against the authority of the states which encroached upon established rights.

The Kurdish press first emerged in 1898. Following the revolution of young Turks in 1908, it began to develop in Constantinople and to contribute to the debate on national problems. After the collapse of the Ottoman Empire (1918), Present Wilson of the United States in his Program for World Peace (Point 12) declared that the non-Turkish minorities of the Ottoman Empire should be granted the right of 'autonomous development'. Section 111, Article 62–63 (Kurdistan) of the Treaty of Sèvres, signed by the allies and the Turkish government on the 10 August 1920, specifically stipulated that the Kurds were to be allowed 'local autonomy'.[37] The Treaty was never enacted because the subsequent War of Independence (waged with Kurdish support) changed the whole situation and enabled Mustafa Kemal to impose different terms at the Treaty of Lausanne, signed in 1923. Meanwhile, Britain had detached the overwhelmingly Kurdish Vilayet of Mosul from Turkey and attached it to Iraq, then a British mandate, in order to seize control of the Mosul oilfields. When the frontiers between Turkey and Syria were drawn up, three areas settled by Kurds were integrated into Syria under French mandate. The division of the Kurdish people was complete. In 1924, a law was passed in Turkey which prohibited the use of the Kurdish language. Since then it has been an offence to publish anything in Kurdish or to teach Kurdish in schools. Kurdish national costume is also banned. The Turkish regime crushed three major national insurrections, in 1925, 1930 and 1937, deprived the Kurds of all rights, and referred to them as mountain Turks. In the meantime, several hundred thousand Kurds were deported to central and western Anatolia. Almost immediately another revolt broke out, this time further north around the foothills of Mount Ararat. It was supported by a new Kurdish liberation organization, Khoyboun, based in Lebanon and Syria, which succeeded in bringing together all the leading Kurdish groups. It was the first time a nationalist organization had assumed so central a role.[38] From 1925 until 1965 Kurdistan was a military area to which foreigners were denied access. Over the last three decades, despite periods of relative political liberalism, the Kurdish national problem, which involves more than 20 per cent of the population, has been mentioned publicly only once. This occurred when the Turkish Workers' Party passed a resolution in 1970 recognizing the existence of the Kurdish people and the legitimacy of its democratic demands. The party was banned as a result.

In 1967 a Kurdish Democratic Party was sent up illegally in Turkey. It had a strong socialist element and was allied to the Turkish Labour Party, which was legal at that time. This alliance brought further military repression to Kurdistan. A short season of liberalism in the Turkish political scene ended in September 1980 as a group of army generals carried out another coup d'état, similar to those of 1960 and 1971. They reinforced martial law in Kurdistan and made it clear that they intended to brook no expression of the Kurdish movement or identity. Since 1980, despite the militarization of Kurdistan, Kurdish political and military activities have continued. The Kurdistan Workers' Party (PKK) and the Revolutionary Democratic Cultural

Association (DDKD) are among several Kurdish political and cultural institutions active in Kurdistan.

The Iraqi Kurdish movements are a continuation of the Kurdish national movement started in the late nineteenth century. When Great Britain annexed the oil-rich Kurdish vilayet of Mosul in 1922, a joint Iraqi–British declaration recognized the Kurds' right to 'form a Kurdish Government within the Iraqi frontiers'. The League of Nations in 1925 awarded the province to the new Arab state of Iraq, on condition that 'regard should be had to the desire expressed by the Kurds that officials of Kurdish race should be appointed for the administration of their country, the dispensation of justice and teaching in the schools, and that Kurdish should be the official language of all these services'.[39]

The award was for twenty-five years. These pledges were not included in the Anglo–Iraqi Treaty of 1930 which gave Iraq its independence. The Kurds became suspicious of the Anglo–Iraqi agreement when they found that there were no written guarantees about Kurdistan. The discovery of oil near Kirkuk in 1927 was a turning point in Kurdish aspiration for an independent state. Because it was the richest deposit discovered anywhere in the world at that time[40] and the concession was dominated by British, American, French and Dutch oil interests, Kurdish nationalists could not expect any sympathy from the West for their movement.

However, the Kurdish struggle for autonomy continued. Sheikh Mahmud Barzanji, who had led the 1919 Kurdish rebellion in Sulaymaniyah, rose again in 1923, and then in 1931. On both occasions he was defeated by Iraqi and British troops. In 1932 another Kurdish leader, Mulla Mustafa Barzani, led a revolt against the Iraqi government which had decided to establish central control over the northern part of Kurdistan. With the help of the Royal Air Force, Barzani was defeated and driven into Turkey. From 1943 to 1945 Barzani led a further revolt and was suppressed with the aid of the Royal Air Force. In his retreat, Barzani decided to join the Mahabad Republic in Iran from which a year later he went into exile in the Soviet Union until 1958.

In 1945, a year after his suppression, the Kurdish Democratic Party was formed by a group of Iraqi Kurdish nationalists and intellectuals, with Barzani as its chairman. Even during his absence, Barzani had remained the Kurdish movement's leader and had become a legendary symbol for the Kurdish people in Iran and Turkey.

After twelve years of exile, Barzani returned to Iraq in 1958 after Abd al-Karim Kassem had overthrown the monarchy. At first the Kurds warmly welcomed the event. The Kurdish Democratic Party was officially recognized. The new Iraqi constitution stated that 'Arabs and Kurds are partners in this homeland', and implied a Kurdish right to autonomy. However, when Kassem had established his power, ignoring all his promises to the Kurds for autonomy, he attempted to change the population balance around the oil-producing region of Kirkuk by deporting the Kurdish people. The good relation between the Kurds and Kassem's regime turned to hostility and conflict was inevitable. On 11 September 1961, the Iraqi army launched a full-scale attack on Kurdistan. Between 1961 and 1968 the armed struggle waged by the Kurds caused the fall of four Iraqi regimes, before the present dominant wing of the Ba'ath came to power in July 1968. Again the new regime signed an agreement with the Kurdish leaders promising autonomy for Kurdistan in all areas of northern Iraq, including the oil-rich Kirkuk area with its Kurdish majority. This agreement was never enacted and the KDP became suspicious of the Ba'ath regime's military activities in Kurdistan. The war continued in 1974 and the Kurdish movement received tactical support from the Shah of Iran and covert support from the United States.[41] After this direct foreign involvement the Kurds suffered again with the Algiers accord (1975) in which the Shah and the Ba'ath regime reached a compromise at the expense of the Kurdish movement. On 15 March the Algiers agreement was made public, Iraq ceded its claim to the whole of the long-disputed Shatt al Arab waterway and accepted the Thalweg Line partition (the middle of the watercourse). Iran and Iraq affirmed the re-establishment of a mutual security agreement along their joint borders and an undertaking to conduct strict control to prevent Kurdish infiltration. Shortly afterwards the Iraqi regime decided to implement a policy of Arabization in the oil-rich and frontier Kurdish areas such as Kirkuk, Khanaqin and Sindjar. Hundreds of thousands of Kurds were deported to the south. Kurdish officials in Kurdistan were replaced by Arab pro-government officials. Towns and villages in parts of Kurdistan were renamed. The villages and woodlands within three kilometres of the Iranian border were razed to the ground.

After this disaster, the Kurdish national movement underwent a profound crisis. The movement split into three factions: the Democratic Party of Kurdistan (provisional leadership); the Patriotic Union of Kurdistan (PUK); and the Democratic Party of Kurdistan (Preparatory Committee).

When the Shah was overthrown in 1979, the different Iraqi Kurdish groups sought Tehran's favours. Both Jalal Talabani of PUK and Masud Barzani, the Mulla Mustafa's son (KDP), publicly supported the Iranian Revolution. In its alliance with the Islamic regime of Iran, the KDP helped Iranian troops against the Iranian Kurdish movement.

Kurdish movements and the Iranian regimes

The relationship between the Iranian Kurds and their governments has always been tense and fragile. During the sixteenth century the Savavid Shahs used the Kurdish tribes to consolidate their rule. They moved Kurds from Kurdistan in the west to Khorasan in the north and north-eastern part of their empire to defend the borders against Usbak invaders. Since the Safavid period during which the Shiite regime was established in Iran, Kurdish Sunnites have suffered religious discrimination. Rezakhan, founder of the Pahlavi dynasty, managed to establish his authority in Kurdistan only by brutal military expeditions. He also moved thousands of Kurds into the central arid part of Iran around Isfahan. During the Second World War the allies occupied Iran, with Russians in the north and British in the south, regardless of the consent of the Iranian authorities. They had one key objective: to dislodge Reza Shah who they suspected would turn his pro-German sympathy into military alliance.[42]

As soon as the central government's control was loosened, the Kurdish nationalists organized a political movement and formed the Komala-i-Zhian-i-Kurd (Committee of Kurdish Rebirth). In the power vacuum they managed to direct their own affairs. In 1945 a new party was founded, the Kurdish Democratic Party (KDP), which in January 1946 declared the Republic of Mahabad and formed a government under the Presidency of Qazi Muhammad. Kurdish became the official language, periodicals appeared and some kind of reforms were introduced. However, as a result of Iranian concessions to the Soviet Union who were interested in the oil of northern Iran, Kurdish aspirations for an autonomous region did not last more than a year. As soon as the Soviet troops retreated from Iran (May 1946) the Iranian army with the support of Great Britain and the United States advanced on Kurdistan and defeated the newly established Mahabad Republic. Qazi Muhammad and several of his colleagues were publicly hanged in Mahabad. For the Kurds this episode was particularly bitter.

After the fall of the Mahabad Republic, the Kurdish Nationalist movement went underground. The acknowledgement of Kurdish identity was forbidden. The Shah's secret police established a security network in Kurdistan and thousands of Kurdish intellectuals and nationalists were imprisoned, tortured and executed. Despite this ruthless suppression the Kurdish Democratic Party continued its campaign until the overthrow of the Shah's regime in 1979.

The downfall of the Shah provided the Kurdish people with new hope for autonomy. The Kurdish political activists organized themselves quickly and took over police and army barracks in the major towns and cities in Kurdistan, confiscated substantial amounts of arms and ammunition, and renewed their demands for autonomy.

Two major Kurdish movements, The Kurdish Democratic Party of Iran (KDPI) led by Abd al Rahman Ghassemlou, and Komala, the revolutionary Marxist organization, consolidated their positions throughout Kurdistan. As they had become suspicious of the Ayatollah Khomeini's attitude towards minorities during his exile, they were not surprised that their demands were rejected by the newly established religious regime in Tehran. Clashes between the Kurdish movements and the Pasdaran (Islamic Revolutionary Guards) occurred. In 1979 the Kurdish revolutionary movements still managed to control more than 80 per cent of Kurdistan. Throughout spring and summer of 1979 the conflict between the Kurds and government forces intensified. Khomeini himself assumed power as Commander-in-Chief of the Armed Forces and launched a full-scale military expedition backed by a 'Fatwa' (a religious ruling by a Muslim cleric considered as binding as a legal decision) against the Kurds. Attacks from the air and on the ground using helicopter-gunships, Phantom aircraft, tanks and artillery forced the Kurdish forces to leave the major towns and cities and retreat to the rural areas. As soon as the government forces reoccupied the Kurdish towns and cities, revolutionary courts were set up by Ayatollah Khalkhali and hundreds of Kurdish youths were executed. As a consequence the Kurdish fighters changed their tactics to guerilla warfare. The conflict continued inside Iran until the outbreak of war between Iran and Iraq and the opening of a front in

Kurdistan. Over 200,000 Revolutionary Guards and regular soldiers occupied every major city, town and village in Kurdistan. The Kurdish forces withdrew and set up guerilla bases in the border area between Iran and Iraq. Since the ceasefire between Iran and Iraq, Kurdish military activities have declined but political activity continues.

The Kurds in Syria

The Kurdish people living in Syria, mostly those who fled from Turkey, are mainly concentrated in three northern frontier areas: Jezireh, Kurd-Dagh and Ain al Arab. The mass migration from Turkey and settlement in these fertile areas caused great tension between the Kurdish communities and the Arab inhabitants. Kurdish national awareness developed here, particularly when Syria became independent, adopted a Pan-Arabist ideology and refused to recognize rights of the Kurds as a minority nation.

In 1957 a group of Kurdish intellectuals, workers and peasants founded the Kurdish Democratic Party (KDP) in Syria, aiming at linguistic and cultural freedom of expression, land reform and a democratic government. The union of Syria and Egypt in the United Arab Republic in 1958 triggered the first round of oppressive behaviour towards the Kurds who were suspected of being in league with the Kurds of Iraq who were demanding autonomy (1961).

In 1962 the Syrian government decided on a plan to establish an 'Arab Belt'. This involved the expulsion of the entire Kurdish population living along the border with Turkey, and the introduction of an Arab population. This plan was drawn up following the discovery of oil at Qaratchok in the middle of Kurdish Jezireh. The plan was partially carried out and many Kurdish peasants left for other parts of Syria, Turkey and Lebanon.

When the socialist Ba'ath Party assumed power in 1963 there was no relief for the Kurds. This resulted partly from the Kurdish revolt against the Ba'ath regime in Baghdad and fears that the uprising might spread. By further persecution and the refusal to implement land reforms in the Kurdish areas the Ba'ath regime in Syria demonstrated that with regard to the Kurds there was no difference between them as a socialist government and other totalitarian regimes in the region. The only exception occurred when two rival regimes needed the assistance of the Kurds. The Ba'ath persecution of the Kurds in Syria began to ease when Hafiz al Assad seized power. He renounced any further implementation of the plan to transfer the Kurdish and Arab population in sensitive areas while Syria had problems with both Iraq and Turkey. Today, the radio broadcasts Kurdish music and the Kurds feel much safer. There is no guarantee however that the present situation will continue.

The impact of the Iranian Revolution on Kurdish national movements

The fall of the Shah and the establishment of the Islamic regime in Iran marked one of the great events of this century. From the Kurdish point of view it was a mixed blessing. On the one hand it provided an opportunity for the Kurds to fulfil their national aspirations for autonomy, but on the other hand the

1980s proved to be a period of extreme misery. Nonetheless, in the upheaval that led to the overthrow of the Shah it was in Kurdistan in particular that democratic slogans were more obvious than religious. There were a number of reasons for this. The Kurdish people are mainly Sunnite Muslims and are thus less vulnerable to the demagogy of the Shiite religious leadership. There was also the national question. The Kurds had been subject to every type of humiliation at the hands of the monarchy of the Shah and his father Reza Khan. They were denied the right to autonomy, the right to study in the Kurdish language and even at times the right to wear Kurdish clothes. This generated deep resentment and the Kurds quite rightly suspected that the Shiite leadership would also refuse to grant them autonomy and their other national rights. Moreover, within the Kurdish movement there were powerful secular trends. The Kurdish Democratic Party of Iran (KDPI), Komala, the Kurdish left-wing organization, and Fedayeen Khalq, the Marxist–Leninist group, were all non-religious organizations.

In addition, the Kurds had hoped for a revaluation which would establish democracy and end despotism. This contrasted with the ambition of the Shiite leadership for a centrally controlled religious government. Despite all the political efforts made by the Kurdish organizations and some secular political groups, conflict between the Kurds and the newly established religious regime of Tehran was inevitable. In August 1979 the Khomeini regime launched an all-out military offensive to assert its authority in Kurdistan. Khomeini ordered this attack as a religious duty or 'Jihad'. The suppression of the Kurds became an obsession with the regime in its drive to consolidate its power. In turn, the Kurdish masses put up ferocious resistance and drew the attention and sympathy of the revolutionaries across Iran. For the first three months the whole of Kurdistan was consumed in warfare. Troops of the regime seized the cities, closed down the press, the schools and the universities and clamped down on the rights of the Kurdish masses. The army and the Revolutionary Guards then set up garrisons and forts on top of the hills surrounding the Kurdish cities, towns and even villages.

Over the past eleven years the Kurds have suffered more than any other Iranian ethnic group or minority. Thousands of Kurdish people have been executed, imprisoned and tortured. Most Kurdish intellectuals have lost their jobs and been put under surveillance or expelled. Many Kurds were among those prisoners executed in the wave of prison killings at the end of 1988.

The Iranian Revolution was regarded by the Iraqi Kurds as possible liberation from the fate imposed on them after the 1975 Algiers Agreement. Talabani's Patriotic Union of Kurdistan (PUK) and Barzani's Kurdish Democratic Party (KDP) both publicly supported the Revolution. Furthermore, the KDP also helped the Iranian forces in their struggle against the Kurdish autonomists in Iran. The alliance of Barzani with Iran caused another major division and the formation of a new splinter group, the Kurdistan Popular Democratic Party (KPDP), led by Sami Abd al Rahman and Nur Shawis. Despite disunity among the Iraqi and Iranian Kurdish organizations, war between the Kurds and their governments continued. It was an absurd situation for the unfortunate Kurdish liberation movements. While the Iranian Kurds were under severe pressure in 1985, the Iraqi Kurds enjoyed Iran's support in their struggle against the Iraqi regime and they succeeded in consolidating their position in more than 80 per cent of Kurdistan. This Kurdish triumph was tempered by the savage Iraqi reaction to the growing Iraqi Kurdish and Iranian threat in the northern sector. In 1987 Iraq adopted more drastic measures with a policy of removing all Kurdish civilians and livestock from the Kurdish countryside. All areas still under Iraqi control during daylight hours were denuded of their population and their villages were razed to the ground. This policy covered areas from Zakho in the north across to Halabja in the south and east of Sulaymaniyah. Over three thousand villages were destroyed and more than 500,000 Kurdish people were deported to detention camps in the desert areas of south and west Iraq. Many others fled as refugees to Iran. Further measures were taken by the Iraqi regime when PUK forces made significant advances around Sulaymaniyah in April 1987. Baghdad used chemical weapons against a number of Kurdish villages in the battle zone. At the beginning of 1988, despite these Iraqi measures, many Kurds remained optimistic about a victory which would bring about the downfall of the Iraqi regime and the fulfilment of Kurdish demands for autonomy.

When, on 16 March 1988, the PUK and the Iranian forces captured Halabja, the Iraqi response was disastrous. The following day it attacked Halabja with chemical weapons and more than 6500 died. Despite international concern no steps were taken to restrain Iraq, which continued to use gas against civilians as well as military targets in different parts of Kurdistan during April and May.

Meanwhile, the ceasefire acceptance by the Iranian government on 22 July 1988 offered the Iraqi regime an opportunity to initiate an all-out offensive on the Kurdish nationalist position using its full potential of air and ground forces and renewal of gas attacks. It gave the Kurds their most dreadful experience. Many civilians evacuated their villages and fled to Iran and Turkey. The continuing Kurdish struggle brought the repeated use of chemical weapons and resulted in the mass movement of the Kurdish population across Turkish and Iranian borders and deportations to detention camps in the desert of south and west Iraq. The conditions of the refugees in the detention camps was very poor with strictly limited time allowed outside camps and inadequate food and health facilities inside. Like Turkey, Iran and Iraq are very reluctant to allow foreign aid workers into their camps. The conditions in the camps were in fact so bad that many refugees preferred to risk the dangers of escape and return to the war zone in Kurdistan. By the end of 1988 the number of Iraqi Kurdish refugees and deportees was as much as one million. Of this figure, about half a million live in the refugee camps in Turkey and Iran and a similar number are detained in the desert camps.

Although reports of the Kurdish genocide have spread round the world, no effective action has been taken against the regimes of Iraq, Iran or Turkey. In this context the Kurdish people have been less fortunate than the oppressed Kuwaitis who became victims of the same oppressor.

The Kurdish question and stability in the region

For centuries the Kurdish people lived in harmony with their neighbouring Arabs, Iranians and Turks. From the moment the Ottoman and Persian Empires demarcated and policed their borders, the Kurds' freedom of movement was jeopardized. The collapse of the Ottoman Empire (1918) gave new hope to all nations in the region, including the Kurds. According to the Sèvres Treaty of 1920 the Kurdish nation was considered an independent national state. At first it was the British who threatened Kurdish independence rights by violating the Sèvres Treaty. Similar injustices have been perpetrated by all states with Kurdish minorities. The Kurds have also been used as pawns in conflicts between the rival states, Iran, Iraq, Syria and Turkey.

Despite all the tragic events, the Kurdish struggle for justice and national rights has continued. Those people who have been driven from their homes and villages, who have lost their families, jobs, and belongings, and are living under constant surveillance either in their birthplace or in the refugee camps or detention centres, have been left with no choice but to fight for peace, freedom and identity. Their struggle will continue until they achieve a measure of cultural, economic and administrative autonomy within their particular state.

Notes

1. Lippman, W. *Thomas, Islam, Politics and Religion in the Muslim World*, p. 32, New York, 1982.
2. Farangi Abdallah, *The PLO and Palestine*, p. 37, Zed Books Ltd., London, 1983.
3. Grollenberg, Lucas, *Palestine Comes First*, p. 29, SCM Press Ltd., London, 1980.
4. Farangi Abdallah, *The PLO and Palestine*, op. cit., p. 50.
5. Wagner, A. 'Balfour Declaration in the Arab–Israeli conflict', p. 110, *International Law*, Berlin, 1971.
6. Mattar, Philip, 'al-Hajj Amin al Husayni and The Palestinian.' *Arab Studies Quarterly*, Vol. 6, No. 4, Fall 1984.
7. Curtis, Michael (ed.), *Religion and Politics in the Middle East*, p. 65, Westview Press, Inc., Boulder. Co., 1981.
8. Obertvoll, John, *Islam, Continuity and Change in the Modern World*, pp. 165–171, Westview Press, Essex, 1982.
9. ibid., p. 165.
10. ibid., p. 168.
11. ibid., p. 169.
12. Tareq Y. Ismael, *The Arab Left*, p. 91, Syracuse University Press, Syracuse, NY, 1976.
13. ibid.
14. Agwani, M.S. *The West Asian Crisis*, p. 7, Meenakshi Prakashan, Begum Bridge, Meerut, India, 1967.
15. Porath Yehoshua, *The Political Organization of the Palestinian Arabs under the British Mandate*, in the Palestinian Arab and Politics, pp. 1–23, Academic Press, Jerusalem, 1975.
16. ibid., pp. 16, 17.

17. Hadawi Sami, *Land Ownership in Palestine*, Arab Information Center, New York, 1961.
18. O'Ballance, Edgar, (1972) *The Arab–Israeli War, 1948*, p. 209, London, Faber.
19. Agwani, *The West Asian Crisis*, op cit., p. 16.
20. Farangi Abdallah, *The PLO and Palestine*, op. cit., p. 90.
21. ibid., p. 91.
22. The world-famous British historian and author of *A Study of History*. Abridgement of v. 1–6, (7–10) by D.C. Somervell, issued under the auspices of The Royal Institute of International Affairs, London.
23. *UNRWA; A Brief History, 1950–1982.* Report of The Commissioner General of the United Nations Relief and Works Agency for Palestinian Refugees in the Near East, General Assembly Offical Records, New York, 1982.
24. Ashkenazi, Abraham, 'Palestine and UNRWA', *Jerusalem Journal of International Relations*, Vol. 12, No. 1, 1990.
25. Farangi Abdallah, *The PLO and Palestine*, op. cit., p. 95.
26. ibid., pp. 100–1.
27. Lesch, Ann M. and Tessler, Mark A. 'The West Bank and Gaza: Political and Ideological Responses to Occupation, in *The Muslim World'*, Vol. LXXVII, No. 3/4, July–October 1987 The Duncan Black Macdonald Center, Hartford, Conneticut, (USA), pp. 229–49.
28. Chaliand, Gerard, 'Minorities without rights'. *People Without a Country: The Kurds and Kurdistan*, pp. 8–17, Zed Press, London, 1982.
29. V. Minorsky's article on the Kurds in the *Encyclopaedia of Islam* Vol. 2, p. 1927, Brill, Leiden, 1960.
30. Ghassemlou, A.R., 'Kurdistan in Iran', in Chaliand (ed.), *People Without a Country: The Kurds and Kurdistan*, op. cit., p. 108.
31. Vanly, Ismet Sheriff, 'Kurdistan in Iraq', in *People Without a Country*, op. cit., p. 153.
32. Kendal, 'Kurdistan in Turkey', in *People Without a Country*, op. cit., p. 48.
33. Kendal, 'The Kurds in The Soviet Union', in *People Without a Country*, op. cit., p. 220.
34. Pelletière, Stephen C., *The Kurds: An Unstable Element in the Gulf*, p. 19, Westview Press, London, 1984.
35. Edmonds, C. J., *Kurds, Turks and Arabs: Politics, travel and research in North-Eastern Iraq 1919–1925.* p. 62. OUP, London, 1957.
36. ibid.
37. Chaliand, 'Minorities Without Rights', in *People Without a Country*, op. cit., p. 12.
38. Short, Martin and McDermott, Anthony, 'The Kurds', *The Minority Rights Group Report*, No. 23, p. 12. 1982.
39. Edmonds, C.J., *Journal of Contemporary History*, op. cit., 1971.
40. 'The Kurds', *Minority Rights Group Report*, No. 23, op. cit., p. 11.
41. Chaliand, *People Without a Country*, op. cit., p. 14.
42. 'The Kurds', *The Minority Rights Group Report*, No. 23, op. cit., p. 16.

Chapter 3
The historical background of Islam

Islam, the religion founded by the Prophet Muhammad, is a truly world religion and like Judaism and Christianity is monotheist with belief in only one god, 'Allah'.

In AD 610, in a bedouin society in the rocky desert peninsula in Arabis, the Prophet Muhammad received his calling from God to preach a new faith, Islam. From the time of Muhammad until the day of the discovery of oil in the early twentieth century, Arabia remained a poor land inhabited by a few rival tribes.

Muhammad was born in AD 570 in Mecca and belonged to an important bedouin tribe known as the Quraysh. By that time Mecca was an oasis and a centre for trade and pilgrimage for Arabs who came long distances to venerate the Ka'aba, an ancient temple for idols. By Muhammad's day the people who came to Mecca brought with them the knowledge of higher religions including Judaism, Christianity and Zoroastrianism. Muhammad seems to have been struck by the contrast between the beliefs of Christians and Jews and those of his own people. At the same time Muhammad was also influenced by tribal conflicts, the development of commerce and foreign influences which all began to undermine the traditional tribal life style. He began to reflect upon the ways of God and their relationship to man. One day, as he worshipped in a cave outside Mecca, he heard a voice telling him to set down the words of God. For the next twenty-two years, he spoke prophetically and preached his new faith. What his followers recorded of his sayings was to become one of the great books of world history, the 'Qur'an'. The Qur'an was put together after his death by Othman, the Prophet's father-in-law and his third successor as Kahlifa (Caliph).

Muhammad proclaimed a belief and a code of behaviour to meet the needs of human societies. Its fundamental concept was that no god was to be worshipped but Allah, the one God; it was uncompromisingly monotheistic. This was a revolutionary belief for his community. According to the new faith, those who remained constant to their old gods would go to hell, a doctrine not very popular among non-Muslim believers of Muhammad's tribe. As a result, many of his tribesman turned on him and became very hostile to his faith.

On 24 September in the year AD 622, Muhammad and his followers left Mecca and went to another oasis about 280 miles to the north, Medina, the city of the Prophet. This migration, or 'Hijrah' as it is called in Arabic, was the turning point in the early stages of Islam. This event, the 'Hijrah', has been regarded as marking the beginning of the Muslim calendar, still in use in the Muslim world.

In Medina, Muhammad organized a new Islamic community and began to introduce and expand his faith through the region. Islam was from the beginning a religion of conquest and Muhammad's own leadership and personality were very important in the early stage of the establishment of the faith. Muhammad succeeded in uniting the rival Arab tribes in Medina and set the stage to subdue those who had opposed him in Mecca and among the tribes nearby. Those who submitted were welcomed into the 'Umma', the brotherhood of believers and those who resisted the new faith were to be annihilated or driven out.

Muhammad died in 632 in Medina. He designated neither an authority to interpret his teaching nor a successor as head of the Islamic community and did not establish a constitution. When he died, the elders of the Medinese community chose Abu Bakr, one of the earliest converts to Islam, as the first Kahlifa, the authorized leader of the Islamic community. When Abu Bakr died, Omar, one of the most powerful and respectable Quraysh leaders was chosen through the consensus of the Medinese community. During the ten years of Omar's leadership the Islamic army conquered the tribes of southern Arabia and headed steadily north. Omar was assassinated and was succeeded by the third Caliph, Othman, who made great efforts to collect the holy writing to form the Qur'an. During Othman's leadership, the Ummayed tribe became very influential and Othman was challenged and killed. Ali, the Prophet's cousin and son-in-law, succeeded. Ali was also challenged by his powerful rivals including Muawiyah, the Ummayed leader, Ayeshah, the Prophet's wife, and the Kharaijites. These last were a group of militant Muslims who opposed Ali's decision to compromise with Muawiyah and they deserted his army. The Prophet's four immediate successors are called the Rashedin Caliphs. They were all related to the Prophet by blood or marriage.

In 661 Ali, the last patriarchal Caliph was killed by the Kharaijites. The office then passed to the Ummayed family who held it for nearly a century. By the time they ceded it to the Abbasid dynasty (750) Islam had remade the map of the world (Figure 3.1). The process of expansion and conquest began soon after the Prophet's death. The Muslims conquered the Sassanid, the Persian Empire and the Byzantine Empire, drove the Romans from Syria and took Jerusalem. They formed an Islamic navy and occupied Cyprus and Carthage in 700. The Berbers were converted to Islam and the whole coast of North Africa was occupied by the Muslims. The Islamic armies had also pushed eastwards to Kabul and in the early eighth century crossed the Hindu Kush and invaded India. At about the same time another Islamic army crossed the Straits of Gibraltar and pushed into Spain. The reason behind such rapid success was probably the Muslim fighters' commitment and devotion to their faith. They believed that death on the battlefield against the infidel would be rewarded by entry to paradise and they thought that they were fighting for God. This made them self-sacrificing and confident in battle.

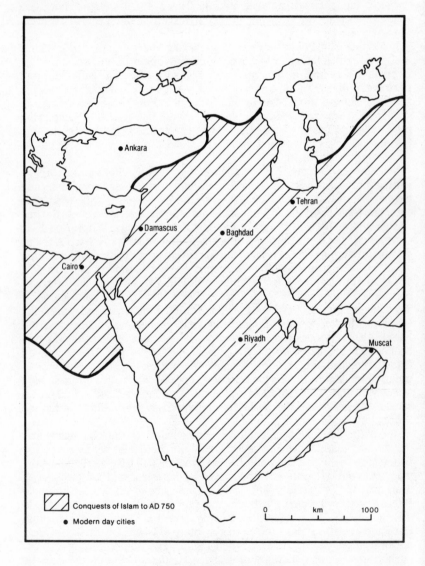

Figure 3.1 Islam in AD 750

The Ummayed Caliphate came to an end when the last Ummayed Caliph was overthrown by Abbassid (750). Abbassid moved the Ummayed seat of the caliphate from Damascus to Baghdad. Baghdad then became the centre of a brilliant civilization. Trade, the arts, science and philosophy flourished, particularly during the legendary Caliphate of Haroun-al-Rashid (765–809). The Abbasid Caliphate lasted until the fall of Baghdad in 1055. From the fall of Baghdad to the rise of Ottoman Turks, about three centuries later, several dynasties appeared. The Islamic world included the Kurdish Ayyubid dynasty based in Egypt which under Saladin (1137–93) created a powerful Islamic empire. Saladin fought the Crusaders with the help of soldier-slaves, called Mamluks, who later governed Egypt and Syria.

Seljuqi Turks also established their own ruling dynasty in Persia (Iran), and Isfahan was their capital. In fact during this period no one could claim to rule all the Muslim world.

The Ottoman Empire

The fall of Constantinople in 1453 was one of the most important events in history. A new world power, the Ottoman Empire, arose and ruled all the Christian states in North Africa, the Balkans and the eastern Mediterranean. The Ottoman Turks became the rulers of the Islamic world.

It began with Osman 1 (1290–1320) who united the Turkish warriors of Anatolia and waged a holy war against Byzantium. The Ottoman advance was stopped at Vienna (1529). In two centuries, the Ottoman Turks had built a much stronger Muslim barrier than any earlier one between Western Christendom and Asia, holding off orthodox Russia to the north and driving deep into the Danube valley.

The Ottomans made great changes in the parts of Europe they ruled. In some places they established an Islamic state while elsewhere they governed in accordance with orthodox Muslim law.[1] The Ottoman Empire comprised multi-racial, multi-religious and multi-cultural societies, with the Islamic religion and Turkish culture firmly dominant. The Ottomans ran the Empire by giving non-Muslim subjects a sort of autonomy or internal self-government within their own community under their own religious leaders. In Europe and wherever else Christianity was practised, language became the mark of nationality. As a result the Ottoman Empire began to decline in the face of Balkan nationalism in the north and the Persian challenge in the east. The European imperial invasion in North Africa had also weakened the Ottoman Empire. In fact, the Ottomans had lost control of most of their territories by 1884. At the end of the Ottoman Empire, a succession of reformist and reactionary regimes presided over a slow modernization, and increasing European domination. Reaction to European influences was twofold; on the one hand techniques, philosophy and ideas associated with liberation and progress were adopted. On the other hand cultural, economic and political domination produced negative reactions and the consequence was a growing feeling of anti-colonialism and a desire for freedom and independence.

The Islamic concept and Islamic division

Islam is an Arabic word meaning 'submission', submission to the will of God. A good Muslim (the word Muslim is a participle from Islam) is one who submits to God, but submission does not mean passivity. Submission to God may require action, social reform and confrontation with evil whenever it is encountered. Although Muslims recognize Jews and Christians as the people of the book, they consider Islam to be the final truth and final revelation, and the Prophet Muhammad to be the last and most perfect Prophet.

The foundations of Islam are the Qur'an, the holy book which was divinely revealed to Muhammad through the archangel Gabriel, and the sunna, the traditions of the Prophet Muhammad and of his pious companions which supplement the Qur'an.

All Muslims, in principle, accept the Sharia, the code of laws that regulate behaviour, social relationships, property and commerce. All Muslims agree that the ideals and duties of the faith are expressed in the so-called Five Pillars of the Faith:

1. The declaration that 'There is no god but the God and Muhammad in the messenger of God.'
2. Ritual prayer five times a day.
3. Zakat, a tithe or tax, representing compulsory almsgiving for the poor.
4. Fasting during Ramadan, the ninth month of the Islamic lunar calendar: no food or drink may be consumed from first light to last light.
5. The pilgrimage (the Hajj) to Mecca, Muhammad's birthplace and the site of the Ka'aka. All Muslims, if they are able, are obliged to make the Hajj once.

All Muslims believe that Islam is a complete system for human existence, universally applicable at all times and places. Islam, as a faith, represents moral strength and cultural continuity. It is understandable that in times of stress, upheaval or social change the banner of the faith is raised and Muslims shelter behind it from the intrusion of alien cultures or political domination.

Although all Muslims share one heritage and have a common base in the faith, they are not united. Different interpretations of the sunna and shari'a give rise to many sects and schools of thought. The earliest division in Islam took place after the death of Prophet Muhammad. When Muhammad died Abu Bakr was chosen as the Prophet's first successor. This decision was disputed by Ali's supporters (the Shiites of Ali) who believed that Ali, as the Prophet's cousin and the father of his grandsons Hassan and Husayn, was the Prophet's legitimate successor. In contrast, the Sunnites, the mainstream of Islam, believed that, following the consensus of their community, Abu Bakr was correctly selected as the Prophet's successor. This dispute over the succession created the major division in the Muslim community. Ali's partisans, the Shiites, have remained loyal to Ali's family to the present day. The Shiites also believe that Ali and his descendants were divinely guided spiritual leaders, called 'Imam', considered by practising believers to be infallible, impeccable and immaculate. They are believed to have ruled in the name of God. The Sunnites, on the contrary, do not believe in Imamate authority, arguing that neither the Qur'an nor the Prophet have specified those who are to be his successors. Therefore, they accepted the temporal authority of chosen caliphs. Sunnites also reject the Shiites' claim that the Prophet had designated Ali as his successor. This controversy has continued over the centuries. The conflicts between Ali's sons, as the Imamate leadership, and their opponents culminated in the massacre of the second Imam (Husain) and seventy-two members of his family and followers by the Yazids (the second Caliph from the Ummayed dynasty) army in Karbala (now a Shiite holy city in Iraq) during Ashura AD 680. (Ashura, the tenth day of the Arabic lunar month of Muharam — 2 June — is an important day of remembrance for Shiites). From the Shiite point of view, Husain and his companions were the innocent victims of a political conspiracy and have been regarded as martyrs ever since.

This incident established a political pretext for Shiites and involved two Islamic doctrines:[2] (a) 'Jihad' (holy war), originally a war waged by Muslims against hostile non-Muslims or for conquest of territory for Islam (Khomeini extended it to mean fighting unacceptable Muslim governments as well); and (b) 'Shahadat' (martyrdom), the Muslims' most noble achievement. Both are effectively Islamic strategies for setting Muslims against enemies of the faith.

Another difference between Sunnites and Shiites is in the status of the leaderships. The Shiite leaders (Ulama) have greater authority than the Sunnite leaders. They are also independent of the government as a result of ample funds from the regular payment of zakat and also income from religious endowments of waqf (the religion's charitable foundation which often controls vast wealth and lands and is usually used for religious and social welfare activities under the Ulama's supervision).

The Shiites Ulama are more centrally organized than their Sunnites counterparts. Because of the Shiite Ulama's independence from governmental control they have been more effective in maintaining their authority and the solidarity of their organization. The Sunnite Ulama are usually devoted to religious matters and are less involved in political affairs than the Shiite Ulama.

The Shiites are more radical on many issues compared with the Sunnites. This is partly because of the Shiite doctrine towards social affairs, politics and religious hegemony, and partly because the Shiite sect is in a minority in the Islamic world. In most Islamic countries in which the Sunnites are in majority, the Shiites have been denied equal opportunities in social and governmental affairs. It can therefore be understood why most uprisings and protests throughout the history of Islam have been initiated by the Shiite sect. The most important difference in the leadership between the Shiites and Sunnites is the role of Mujtahed (juristic), the authority of specialists in religious learning. In Shiite, the juristic principle differentiates religious authority and creates a basis on which a hierarchical authority is established alongside the political authority, but independent of it.

The rise of fundamentalism

Centuries of war, poverty and colonial domination have suppressed Islamic culture and drained the political strength of most Muslim communities. At the same time, Islamic ideology has shown its potential to renew and reassert itself against competing ideologies and alien influences. The establishment of the colonial system in the territories of the defeated Ottoman Empire brought to the fore anti-Western feeling in all Muslim communities. This feeling was gradually reinforced over the decades after the First World War by additional phenomena which can be summarized:

(a) After the collapse of the Ottoman Empire in the First World War (1918) Western colonial powers, specifically Britain and France, occupied the whole Islamic Arab world, and this allowed Western culture to penetrate and influence every aspect of traditional Muslim daily life — social, cultural, economic and political. This colonial domination resulted in an Islamic resurgence and the development of liberation ideology. The idea of Islamic liberation became more popular among Muslim intellectuals when nationalism failed to prevent the establishment of the Jewish State of Israel.

(b) Despite the establishment of independent statehood in the Islamic countries, the social conditions still remain generally unchanged. If there had been any change, it was inimical to Islamic values. The failure of the ruling governments to carry out adequate reforms had created an ideological vacuum that fundamentalists attempted to fill with Islamic values.

(c) The establishment of a Jewish state in the heart of the Muslim world (1948), successive military defeats and the consequences of those defeats, particularly the loss of Islamic territory, and the creation of further homelessness, produced shock waves, humiliation and anger, especially among the Arab nations. As a result, not only were Israel and its Western capitalist supporters blamed, but the competence of the Arab government was in question. In this context the resurgence of Islamic fundamentalism was quite understandable.

(d) In 1955 the United States and Britain exploited the Islamic religion for their own political purposes by sponsoring the Baghdad pact as an anti-communist barrier. They brought the major regional Islamic states, Pakistan, Iran, Iraq and Turkey, into a single political pact to counter the influence of the Soviet Union and to prevent the spread of communist ideology in the region. At the same time, the Islamic nature of the pact was canalized to combat the Pan-Arab nationalist regimes of the region more tolerant toward Muslim fundamentalist activities.

(e) The immediate consequence of the decline of Pan-Arab ideology and the overshadowing of nationalism in most Arab states was the rise of Islamic fundamentalism.

(f) The internal policy adopted by most Islamic countries had produced different impacts on the various sectors of society. These can be interpreted as class discrimination, social discrimination or even minority religious discrimination. For example, the Shiite sect in Lebanon had been deprived of economic and social privileges by both the Christians and the Sunnite Muslim sect for a long time. The natural reaction of the Shiites was rebellion. Militant tendencies or terrorist activities were adopted by this group as tactics to achieve their religio-political ambitions.

(g) The concerns of the United States and its European partners about the stability of the Persian Gulf states threatened by socialist and nationalist movements in the region resulted in the formation of an Islamic pact by Iran and Saudi Arabia using Islamic trends to combat Nasser's growing popularity (after 1955) as a nationalist and socialist. The consequence was a resurgence of exploited Islamic values.

(h) Changes in some of the traditional structures of society including the liberation of women did not sit well with religious attitudes. Therefore, women's activities in society became a major issue of controversy between religious fundamentalist leaders and those who sought a new vision of society. Reaction to this issue was expressed in the most radical form of the Islamic religion.

(i) Modernization and modern ideology had tended to result in the disintegration of old societal institutions and traditions. The effects of the growing sense of insecurity and alienation in the Muslim world are expressed by religious resurgence to protect traditional culture and established institutions. The nature of the modernization process and the authoritarian way in which it had been carried out in the Islamic world contributed to the emergence of Muslim fundamentalism. This is because the process of modernization had generally been carried out in an unbalanced and unfair manner with regard to the distribution of economic and social benefits among Muslim communities. In addition, most of the leaders of Islamic states had used the modernization process to legitimize and secure their own positions as progressive rulers. Thus those who remained deprived and whose life had been disrupted by the effects of modernization had resorted to the traditional values of the Islamic religion.

(j) The establishment of an Islamic regime in Iran (1979) triggered a wave of Islamic fundamentalism not only in the region, but echoed throughout the Muslim world. The assassination of Sadat, the revolts in Syria and Saudi Arabia, sabotage and threats in Kuwait and Bahrain, and unrest in Algeria, Morocco, the Philippines and India are all a reflection of a new stage of Islamic resurgence.

Muslim Brotherhood (Ikhwan al-Muslemeen)

One of the main groups of fundamentalists is the Muslim Brotherhood (Muslim Brethren), founded in 1928 by a young Muslim fundamentalist teacher, Hassan al-Banna, in the city of Ismailia, an Egyptian city that was controlled by the Suez Canal Company, a Franco-British concern.

The Brotherhood undertook a large-scale programme of publishing books, magazines and newspapers. The founder of the Brotherhood joined the al-Manar group, which in a sense could be regarded as the founder of Islamic fundamentalism in this century. Hassan al-Banna was formally chosen as the Supreme Guide of the Muslim Brotherhood Organization in 1938. While the Brotherhood continued its educational, social and religious activities, it became increasingly concerned with, and an influential factor in, the political life of Egypt. Although Banna was intellectually a combination of reformist and political activist he conceived his mission as providing a more comprehensive vision of Islam. For Banna, the Islamic ideal was represented by the first generation of Muslims. For him the difference between current Islamic societies and the true Islamic society was the cause of the decadence in the Muslim community (Umma). The mission of the Brotherhood, therefore, was to 'lead Mankind towards truth, call humanity to the path of goodness and illuminate the entire world with the light of Islam'.[3]

As a result of his activities, Banna was imprisoned by the British authorities in the early 1940s. After his imprisonment, Banna founded a more secret 'sub-group' within the Brotherhood known as the 'Secret Apparatus'. This was in fact an efficient military wing by which he could impose his Islamic philosophy in the Islamic communities. This militant group was originally intended to lead a powerful uprising (the campaign of terror was to become a model for future fundamentalist movements in the Middle East). Yet, because of its size, organization, array of activities and the discipline of its members, the Brotherhood made its influence felt on the national political scene, particularly after the Second World War. The Secret Apparatus undertook its own campaign.[4]

Following several assassinations of political figures in Egypt, Banna's organization was formally banned in 1948 and Banna himself was executed in 1949. Despite its failure to fulfil its Supreme Guide's ambitions to seize power and establish itself as an Islamic regime in Egypt, the movement succeeded in influencing many revolutionary groups and movements which aimed to bring about changes in Egypt and other Islamic states in the Middle East. Although there was early cooperation with the free officers group which brought Nasser to power, once the Brotherhood started its campaign against Nasser's internal policy, tension developed which remained until 1970 when Nasser died. The conflict between the Muslim Brotherhood and Nasser's regime resulted in the establishment of a more serious underground militant organization which spread its ideology throughout the region and gradually the whole Muslim world.

During the period from 1970 to 1981, when it resumed its violent activities, the Muslim Brotherhood played an important role in Egyptian political life. This period is marked with a mixture of peaceful coexistence and compromise, on the one hand, and confrontation between the Brotherhood and Anwar al-Sadat, the President of Egypt and Nasser's successor, on the other.

Once Sadat took power, he was faced with two important political and social situations. Firstly, after unsuccessful wars with Israel, and very costly projects such as the Aswan Dam, Sadat faced serious economic and social problems. In response he made radical changes in both internal and external policies. These included welcoming Western investors, improving relationships with the conservative, rich Arab states including Saudi Arabia and Kuwait, and negotiating peace with Israel. As a consequence the Sadat regime was criticized by various factions inside and outside Egypt. Internally he was under constant threat by Nasserist and socialist groups. Externally he was condemned by radical and even conservative Arabs when he signed the Peace Accords with Israel. Secondly, the position of Sadat with regard to the Muslim Brotherhood was in calculated balance until 1978. Sadat used religion and religious groups, specifically the Muslim Brotherhood, as a curb upon the ambitions of the radical left and nationalists and their attempts to exploit the situation. Therefore the Brotherhood adopted a strategy of peaceful coexistence with Sadat.

From 1978 to 1981, this peaceful coexistence turned into confrontation as a result of (a) the Camp David Peace Treaty with Israel; (b) the increasing gap between the classes, high inflation rates and socio-economic corruption which provided a fertile ground for the activities of fundamentalists; and (c) the Iranian Revolution and the Khomeini phenomenon which gave the Brotherhood immense confidence and a new hope for the possibility of establishing an Islamic regime in Egypt. As a result, the Brotherhood became the group which posed the most serious threat to the Sadat regime.

By 1979, the increasing militancy of Islam in Iran was also in evidence in Egypt, especially among the university students, rural people and low-ranking military. By 1980, sympathy and support for Muslim militant groups had increased and every sign indicated that a clash between Sadat and the militant Muslim association was inevitable. By 1981 the situation created by Sadat and the Muslim fundamentalist and other opposition groups finally produced the outcome which created the second big shock in the Middle East, after the Iranian Revolution of 1979: the assassination of Sadat at a pro-Islamic military parade. Despite serious restrictions which followed, the assassination of Sadat raised the morale of the fundamentalist groups.

Among the several Muslim fundamentalist groups known as al-Jamiat-al-Islamiya which operate in Egypt, besides the Brotherhood, two are particularly important. The first one is known as al-Takfir, Wal-Hijra, the strongest and perhaps the best-organized of the other groups. This group appears to have been formed in the early 1970s and its first appearance as a political force was marked in 1974 when a group of its members participated in the attack on the army's military technical college in Cairo. It has since been involved with rival organizations in political violence. The other important group is Al-Jihad which organized the Sadat assassination and fought with the security forces in the city of Asyut. Among the hundreds of Al-Jihad who were put on trial in 1981 were members of the Presidential guard, the military intelligence and the security service, university students, teachers and lawyers.

Sadat's successor, Hosni Mubarak, confronted the demands of the same opposition groups and interests which played such an important role in Sadat's downfall. The fundamental problem still remains and has, to some extent, worsened.

Islamic resurgence in Iran

The Iranian Revolution of 1978–9 and the establishment of an Islamic fundamentalist regime was a social and political event that exploded in the Middle East, leaving in its wake new and heightened aspirations, fears and insecurities, both in Iran and throughout the Muslim world. It is certainly one of the most important events and controversial phenomena in the region since the Second World War. It is important because of its effects and consequences. It is controversial because of its support for all Muslim militant movements. In order to be objective about the essence of the Islamic resurgence in Iran, it is important to look at the background of Islamic political activities since the beginning of this century.

Iran's Revolution is generally seen as marking the resurgence of Shiaism, which is a deep-rooted belief among the majority of Iranians. Apart from the Kurdish, Baluchi and Turkman minorities which are Sunni, the rest of the nation are mainly Jaafari Shiite. Shiaism has been the official religion of the Persian state (from 1924 and with the rise of the Pahlavi, the name of the state was changed from Persia to Iran) since 1502 and as the established faith it became structured, hierarchical and independent of governments. This independence provided a good basis for the Shiite leadership to exercise its authority.

During the twentieth century, Iran has experienced the role of the Islamic religions and their leadership in the institutions of the state. In this context the Shiite Ulama (the body of learned advisers empowered to pronounce religious rulings) have played an important role in Iran's political scene. They, with the support of bazaar merchants, led a successful protest against the Shah's grant of the tobacco monopoly to a foreigner in 1891; they were responsible for advising Reza Shah (the founder of the Pahlavi dynasty) to set up a monarchy rather than a republic in 1924. Ayatollah Kashani, one of the most powerful and influential Shiia leaders in recent Iranian history, gave strong support to Mohammad-e-Mosaddeq, the Iranian nationalist and Prime Minister during nationalization of Iranian oil (1951–2). Ayatollah Khomeini was responsible for the agitation and violent protest against the Shah's land reforms in 1963. He also led the fundamentalist movement that overthrew the Shah's regime in 1979.

This proves that in Iran militant Shiites have long been active and the Ulama have always been involved in the major social and political events. The fundamental issue involved has been opposition to foreign and secular influences. Because of the Ulama's financial independence from the state, it has been able to act with great freedom.

The role of the religious leadership declined and the Ulama were suppressed for more than fifteen years when Reza Shah ruled the country. After the removal of the Reza Shah by the British forces in 1941, the religious activists reappeared. A new militant fundamentalist organization, the Fedaiyyan-e-Islam, emerged and played an important role in a turbulent period of Iran's modern history. The new revivalists, who reflected the ideological principles of Shiite fundamentalism, carried out several political assassinations and created an environment of fear and terror among the leading political figures. The Fedaiyyan-e-Islam was founded by a young religious teacher named Navabe Safavi in 1945 as a militant Shiite group dedicated to enforcing of Islamic laws and opposing secularism and foreign cultural and political influences. Safavi recruited his followers from the lower middle class and the urban working class, his role dedicated to creating an slamic society and state.

Despite some criticism from the traditional religious leadership, Fedaiyyan enjoyed the sympathy of prominent religious leaders such as Ayatollah Abu al Qaseme Kashani, one of Mosaddequ's supporters and Ayatollah Ruholla Khomeini, later the leader of the Islamic Revolution of Iran. Both Kashani and Khomeini as Shiite religious leaders and leading political figures played a decisive role in Iran's modern history.

Despite his early support, Kashani later began to oppose Mosaddeq and all liberal and nationalist movements. He was intolerant of the Communist Party and other secular organizations. The 1953 coup d'état arranged by the CIA and British Intelligence which deposed Mosaddeq and returned the Shah to the throne had Kashani's support. The re-establishment of the Pahlavi monarchy in 1953 was followed by restrictions of all political activities, including the Fedaiyyan organization.

For more than two decades, dictatorship and Western political, economic and cultural intervention laid the foundations for Iran's 1979 Revolution and the resurgence of fundamentalist activities. In 1963, when the Shah proclaimed the White Revolution, Khomeini, the most influential militant religious leader, protested and put his philosophy into practice, mobilizing his followers against the programme by boycotting the referendum to which the programme was subject. This was probably the most serious direct challenge to the Shah's authority since Mosaddeq's national movement. Despite the severe suppression of anti-Shah demonstrations in Tehran and Qom, the holy city to the south of Tehran, Khomeini succeeded in persuading the hard core of the Shiite fundamentalists. This provided a new vision different from that of the Shah who wanted to Westernize Iran and create a powerful imperial state. As a result, several underground religious and Marxist groups emerged and challenged the Shah's authority.

Following the Tehran and Qom incidents, Khomeini was arrested and sent to exile in Turkey and from Turkey to Najaf in Iraq. Khomeini in exile (1964–79) continued his campaign against the Shah and elaborated the doctrine of an Islamic state. In the final stage of his struggle against the Shah, Khomeini declared the Shah's regime illegitimate. This was an old and influential religious tactic which shook the regime. Khomeini's message was simple and clear: 'The Shah has no right to be on his throne; the government belongs to the Hidden Imam (Mahdi) who bears the title of Saheb-e-zaman (Lord of the time), and in his absence government must be exercised by his vicars (Nayeb-e-Imam) or a "Mojtahed" who is qualified to head the Islamic state.' The Khomeini issue coincided with the uprising in universities initiated by various revolutionary groups and intellectuals, including writers, poets, lawyers, academics, students and political organizations such as Fedaiyyan-e-Khalq (Marxist), Mujahedin-e-Khalq (Young Enlightened religious group), the National Front, and other secular and religious groups. Khomeini paid tribute to the movement by sending revolutionary taped messages from exile to mobilize his followers.

When Khomeini took power, he gradually revealed his doctrine of creating an 'Islamic state'. Within less than a year most of the revolutionary activists became his opponents and the struggle for sharing power became imminent. The democratic revolution had changed to a religious revolution. All other revolutionary activists were deprived of power. A new violent fundamentalist group 'Hezb-Allah' organized by the clergy suppressed all democratic demonstrations and every form of resistance to Khomeini's doctrine. Hezb-Allah played a crucial part in the establishment of Khomeini's fundamentalism by attacking the headquarters of the opposition organizations, setting fire to the bookshops and printing houses of newspapers critical of the religious dictatorship, and attacking all opposition meetings and demonstrations. Hezb-Allah later became the strong backbone of the regime and set itself up as the true defender of Khomeini's doctrine. In the meantime, the Fedaiyyan-e-Islam was reorganized by its former members and its leaders became key figures in Khomeini's regime. They included the notorious Assadulla Layvaidi and Sadeq KhalKhali, who executed thousands of opposition activists and revolutionaries.

After suppressing all opposition groups and organizations who had a role in the revolution, and having secured his authority, Khomeini's prime goal was to export the Islamic Revolution to the other Islamic states. It began with a massive propaganda campaign against the conservative rulers of Islamic countries and attempts to incite their Shiite residents to action. Iraq, Lebanon, Bahrain and Saudi Arabia were the main targets. Khomeini had openly emphasized that the Islamic Revolution sought to convert the governments of Muslim states to the 'Islamic outlook that he espouses'. In a speech to a group of ambassadors he stated:

> What we want for all countries amd all governments is what has happened here, the awakening that has occurred in Iran. The distance this puts between the people and the super powers, the way we cut their hands from our resources . . . you are giving away the wealth of the Muslims; those things that should be used in the interest of the Muslims, to non-Muslims and for nothing.[5]

Khomeini started attacking the Western style of life, modernization in general, the Western school of thought and secularism. His prime non-Islamic targets were America and Israel; the Soviet Union, Great Britain and other Western powers were also condemned.

The phenomenon of Khomeinism was, however. treated as a direct threat by almost every Islamic state from Indonesia in the Far East to Morocco in North Africa. Since 1981, in every radical Islamic movement, portraits of Khomeini and translations of his thought in the local language have been an essential part of provocation. It became evident that Khomeini's appeal was not limited to Shiites only. The Sunnite Muslim fundamentalists also adopted his slogans in their efforts to mobilize mass support. Militant Muslims everywhere became a potential political challenge to the traditional Islamic regimes. It is a general concept that in countries in which the proletarian parties and democracy are suppressed, religion and religious emotions provide strongest motives for the masses to express their social anxiety and to protest. The existence of such emotions forced some of the Muslim countries to reintroduce the Islamic laws in order to accommodate the new mood of Islamic militancy initiated by Khomeini, while others relegated religion to the spiritual realm so that its influence should not spill over into the political arena. According to one estimate,[6] the number of mosques in many Gulf states tripled in number. While some countries have been seeking a compromise, others have been entering into regional security agreements.

Today, Khomeinism and Hezb-Allah, as a way of life and belief and supported by an army of Shiite fundamentalists, are active not only in Iran, but also in Lebanon, Iraq, Turkey, India, the Philippines and oil-rich states in the Persian Gulf. Khomeini advocated not only the resurgence of the Islamic militant tendency in Iran, but the revival of the Islamic fundamentalism throughout the Muslim world.

The Shiite resurgence in Lebanon

Among the many religious communities of Lebanon, the Shiites are probably the most oppressed. Because of the suppression under which the Shiites have lived for a long time, they maintain a tradition of opposition to the dominant authorities, and of being receptive to revolutionary ideas.

When Palestinian refugees moved to Lebanon and started their campaign against Israel, they benefited from the presence of partisans among the Shiite community in southern Lebanon and in the suburbs of Beirut. The Palestinian guerrilla activities against Israel in south Lebanon and Israel's reprisals in the Shiite villages moved the whole Shiite community to create a new element on the Lebanon political scene. At the time Nasserism, as an Arab socialist ideology, was also very popular. It was not a coincidence that in 1967 Iran sent an ambitious Mullah 'Mossa Sadr' to Lebanon to establish a Shiite fundamentalist organization to confront the influences of Nasser and the secular Palestinian groups. The Lebanese Shiites had always looked to Iran as a source of inspiration and moral support. Thus Sadr's arrival in Lebanon on a sacred mission did not provoke any surprise and he quickly became the leader of the Shiites who formed the largest community in Lebanon and he assumed the title of Imam, or leader, of the community of the faithful.[7] In 1968, he set up the Shiite organization Amal (hope), and later, in 1971, he ordered the training of 'volunteers' as armed guardians of the faith.

It was Iran, together with Libyan financial help and the assistance of various Palestinian Liberation Organization groups which made possible the creation of the Shiite guerrillas who later played the most important part in Lebanon's social and political life. Among the trainees were revolutionary Iranians who later made themselves available to Sadr's army. One of them was Mostafa Chamran, who became the first Minister of Defence of the Islamic Republic of Iran with responsibility for organizing the Iranian Revolutionary Guards, the major force in the Khomeini regime.[8] The Amal organization was gradually turned into a fighting force by Chamran. The new organization attracted a large number of young Shiites, including several

Western-educated militants. One of them, Nabih Berri, was to become a prominent figure.

During the 1970s, all rival armed groups in Lebanon were engaged in the power struggle, the Amal organization having built up its strength as a result of concerns from different sources, including Iran, Syria, Libya and Israel. Each sought their own interests through the powerful Shiite organization in the power struggle in Lebanon. Israel wanted the Palestinian forces away from southern Lebanon and only Amal was capable of carrying out this task. Syria regarded Amal as a potential force capable of counterbalancing the influence of the pro-Egyptian Sunnite Muslims. Iran and Libya were seeking a foothold in Lebanon to fulfil their ambitions.

After the Iranian Revolution, the Amal organization, heavily influenced by Khomeini's propaganda, began to commit itself as the vanguard of an Islamic revolution in Lebanon and became the main breeding ground for Shiite terrorism.

Following the mysterious disappearance of Mossa Sadr, the Amal leadership changed and Berri was elected as President of the Amal Command Council in 1980. In 1982, Hussain Mussawi, a member of the Command Council of Amal, acccused the leadership of compromising the organization by having dealings with the Christian Falange and the Israeli invaders, and urged a reorientation backed by Iranian support with the goal of an 'Islamic Revolution'. Mussawi broke away from the mainstream of Amal and moved to Baalbeck to lead his partisans and create a new faction 'the Islamic Amal'. Meanwhile, the mainstream of Amal, led by Berri, enjoyed Syrian approval. The radical break-away faction led by Mussawi received the full support of the Iranian Islamic regime.

However, within the Shiite ranks, Berri started to face a growing challenge from religiously motivated groups, the Islamic Amal and other groups, with similar visionaries, who drew much of their inspiration from Khomeini. The trend which looks set to continue is partly explained by Amal's reluctance to join the resistance in the south, in spite of assaults by Israel and South Lebanon Armies (SLA) on Shiite villages and, most important, by the failure to give Amal a coherent ideology beyond a rather amorphous Shiite identity.[9]

The Hezballah phenomenon in Lebanon

There are several schools of Shiite revolutionary thought. The most important is the one in the Islamic Republic of Iran which is based on Ayatollah Khomeini's concept of revivalist Islam. The other adherents of Khomeinism include the Hezb-ad Dawa al-Islamiyya of Iraq and the Hezballah in Lebanon.

Hezballah, as the most important element in the Shiite political spectrum in Lebanon, is in fact an Islamic radical revivalist tendency rather than an organization. At the symbolic level it provides a new vision of the Shiite movement, struggling against all aspects of a non-Islamic way of life. It is against both the alienation of the Shiite masses and non-Islamic governments.[10]

In Hezballah's vision the Shiite state that found its fulfilment in Iran should be duplicated in Lebanon. The Hezballah phenomenon in Lebanon arises out of the accumulated resentments of several decades. It was Israel, by attacking the Shiite villages and later the occupation of southern Lebanon, that awoke the sleeping giant of anger and indignity which was formed in the shape of Hezballah.[11] This has given the Shiites a strong sense of self-respect and martyrdom, which Hezballah has maintained through its leadership against Israel and all Western interests, particularly those of America, Great Britain and France, in Lebanon. The essence of the Hezballah movement drew heavily on the Shiite religious heritage, with its symbolism, its rituals, its values and its heroes. While Shiite ideology had always been the principal Islamic ideology of social protest, Hezballah attempted to reinterpret these symbols to give contemporary meaning to the rituals and to draw out their implications for the current struggle. They use religious symbolism and the Islamic code to legitimize their socio-political action and activities. Hezballah uses religious symbolism not only to evoke the collective memory of the community but also to encourage them into action. Hezballah masterminded a new stage of violence in the history of the power struggle or mass protest against injustice, but it was a challenge with socio-religious motivations.[12] It was a challenge against all internal rivals including the Amal organization and a challenge against all external powers, except the Iranian Islamic regime, seeking influence in Lebanon. It was a challenge against the super powers, and it was fervent in its hostility to all Western ideologies and the Western style of life. This was demonstrated by attacks on public places such as cinemas, nightclubs, casinos and intolerance to Western clothes.[13]

By 1986, Shaikh Muhammad Hussein Fadhl-Allah, who was regarded as the most distinguished scholar among the Lebanese Shiites, established himself as the spiritual guide of the Lebanese branch of Hezballah. Fadhl-Allah, basing his ideas on Khomeini's pronouncements, set the course for a certain type of action by Shiites in Lebanon. Those who follow his line are all considered members of Hezballah. Thus, it is almost certain that more than half a dozen Shiite groups and cell organizations carry out their activities under the umbrella of Hezballah.[14] They are independent of each other but have close relationships and enjoy cooperation. Among these, al Amal al Islami (Islamic Amal), led by Hussain Mussawi, is probably the largest and best-organized group. Western intelligence is of the opinion that many of the terrorist attacks, including suicide missions, and the kidnapping and holding of Western hostages have been carried out by Mussawi and his associated groups, including Islamic Jihad (holy war) and the Islamic Justice Organization. All these terms are considered as a cover for a variety of operational terrorist groups within the Hezballah.

Notes

1. Roberts, J.M., *Different World*, pp. 114–15, Book Club Associates, London, 1980.

2. Taheri Amir, 'The inside story of Islamic terrorism', *Holy Terror*, Sphere Books Limited, London, 1987.
3. Hassan al-Banna, *What Is Our Message?*, p. 10, (publisher unnamed) Karachi, 1968.
4. ibid., p. 341.
5. *Iran Times*, 31 October 1980, p. 14.
6. Bill, J.A., 'Islam, Politics and Shiism in the Gulf', *Middle East in Sight*, Vol. 2, January/February 1984, pp. 3-12.
7. Taheri Amir, *Holy Terror*, op. cit., p. 65.
8. ibid.
9. McDowall, David, Lebanon: 'A Conflict of Minorities', *The Minority Rights Group Report*, No. 61, London, 1983.
10. Taheri Amir, *Holy Terror*, op. cit., pp. 120-2.
11. ibid.
12. ibid.
13. ibid.
14. ibid.

Chapter 4
Geopolitics and oil

The geopolitics of energy began with oil. Until the early part of the twentieth century, coal was the dominant fuel and geopolitical problems were hardly considered. In general, the major industrial countries had their own sources of coal and very little entered world trade. Bunkering points were established along the main sea-lanes to serve shipping, but fuel vulnerability was not identified as a major threat. Furthermore, the global order was more tightly controlled by the Great Powers and local conflict tended to bring a swift response in the form of gunboat diplomacy. Should major supply problems have arisen, the world distribution of coal is far more even than that of oil and alternative sources could have been relatively easily located.

With the adoption of oil as the major energy source for modern economies and, in particular, for transport, the entire picture changed radically. Since the Second World War, the developed economies have become increasingly dependent upon Third World, politically unstable, sources. The number of major suppliers has always been limited and the result has been the development of a few strategic arteries, linking these sources with the consumers. Thus, to supply vulnerability has been added the problems of defending sea-lanes. Furthermore, as the resources are exhausted, the geopolitical problems will become more acute. At the focus of attention, of course, is the Middle East and in particular the Persian/Arabian Gulf, the region which dominates world reserves. Dependence upon the Middle East has fluctuated in general and has also varied from country to country, but, by the early part of the next century at the latest, it will again predominate.

In a speech delivered on 14 November 1974, Henry Kissinger identified oil as 'the world's most strategic commodity'. This remark was made in the context of the huge oil requirement in the developed world and the extremely marked supply concentration, basically in the developing world. The speech was made at the time of the first oil 'shock'. There followed a further shock in 1979–80, while the greater part of the 1980s experienced a quiescent period, the effects of which are discussed later. At the end of the 1980s, the situation has changed yet again with the break-up of the Warsaw Pact and what seems to be the incipient dismantling of the Soviet Union itself. The post-war, bipolar world, dominated by East–West confrontation, has been swept away. The more obvious confrontation now is between the 'have' and 'have not' nations, on a North–South axis. It follows from this that, given the relative states of development of North and South, the most likely subject of contention will be resources. Indeed, no sooner had the new era of resource geopolitics been generally accepted by international relations experts than a prime example occurred with the Iraq–Kuwait crisis of 1990 and the attendant Western response.

Historical development

In the first book to appear on the event, *Saddam Hussein and the Crisis in the Gulf* by Judith Miller and Laurie Mylroie,[1] it is stated that: 'oil is the modern world's heroin. The pleasure it provides fuels a way of life no other energy source can satisfy so plentifully and so cheaply. Efforts to kick the habit have proved halfhearted, painful and unsuccessful.' The history of oil in the Middle East is the history of a power struggle with the ascendancy passing from the major oil companies to the producer countries, then to OPEC and, finally, to the entrepreneurs and the stock market 'high rollers'. The colonial approach has been succeeded by econo-colonialism, the extreme effects of which are being felt in the upper Gulf today. It is a sorry saga of greed, collusion and perfidy which, interwoven with Arab nationalism and burgeoning Islamic fundamentalism, has produced the backcloth for recurrent Middle Eastern crises.

While Iraq and Iran are highly dependent upon oil, the states of the Arabian Peninsula, with the exception of Yemen, exist because of oil. As a result of oil discoveries, they were encouraged, usually with the active participation of the West, to declare themselves separate entities. The demarcation of boundaries, both onshore and offshore, has been crucially influenced by the perceived limits of oil and gas fields. The wealth resulting from such discoveries has brought about an almost uncontrolled rush to modernity, which has exacerbated all the many differences already existing in Middle Eastern society. In particular, the gaps between wealthy and poor and between old and young have been greatly widened. In response to the question as to whether such vast and rapidly accumulated fortunes have been inimical to the Arab way of life, the only possible reply must be a further question, posed in the context of the modern Gulf states: what is the Arab way of life?

The oil industry is now so vast that its network of interrelationships completely enmeshes the world, affecting every country. It is thus the only truly global industry. Furthermore, as the major areas of production and consumption tend to be separate, oil also dominates world trade. There are many focal points of this industry such as the headquarters of the oil multinationals and the stock markets of New York, London and Tokyo, but the major focus of increasing importance is the Persian/Arabian Gulf.

The vast structure is, however, of very recent origin. Oil was only discovered in the Middle East at the beginning of the twentieth century, and even as late as the early 1940s the area produced only 5 per cent of the world's oil. By 1950, this had become 15 per cent, by 1960, 25 per cent, and by 1979, the peak reached so far of 39 per cent was achieved. From the start, the United Kingdom was pre-eminent and the Anglo-Persian Oil Company was established in 1909 to exploit a concession granted by the government of Iran to prospector William d'Arcy, described by some sources as a New Zealander and by others as British. The concession was typically huge, covering the whole of Iran, apart from its five northern provinces.

The first major stimulus to the embryonic industry came when Winston Churchill, as First Lord of the Admiralty, took the decision in 1911 to change the fuel of the ships of the Royal Navy from coal to oil. From this period until the early 1970s, the oil world was controlled by initially seven and later, eight major international corporations. The original 'seven sisters' were Standard Oil of New Jersey (later Esso/Exxon); Royal Dutch Shell (Shell); British Petroleum (BP); Gulf Oil (Gulf); Texas Oil (Texaco); Standard Oil of California (Socal/Chevron); and Mobil Oil (Mobil). Later, Compagnie Française des Pétroles (CFP) gained sufficiently in importance to be added to the list of 'Majors'. Even by the late 1960s, these Majors controlled almost three-quarters of the major world oil industry and over 80 per cent of that in the Middle East. Their iron grip had been loosened somewhat during the 1950s and 1960s by the appearance of the so-called 'Independents', which consisted of approximately thirty relatively small corporations, some private and some state-owned. Included among these were Phillips Petroleum, Getty and Ente Nazionale Idrocarbui (ENI). These newcomers offered better terms to the producer countries and were influential in breaking the hegemony of the Majors. However, they merely modified what was, effectively, oil imperialism. Developments in the producing countries of the Middle East were shaped almost entirely by the international oil corporations, fully supported by their home governments: American, British, Dutch and French. Even where the producers had full political control over their own territory, they were denied economic independence. Furthermore, they lacked the necessary skills and were indeed discouraged from acquiring them. The Majors controlled production, refining and marketing and left no room for local initiative. Moreover, the means used to gain such an ascendency were often highly questionable. This was well illustrated by al-Otaiba in *OPEC and the Petroleum Industry:*[2] 'Iraq, for instance, was threatened with dismemberment of the Mosul Province from its territory unless the government agreed to grant a concession to the then Turkish Petroleum Company, later renamed the Iraq Petroleum Company (IPC).' Threats were not limited solely to the producer countries. Among the consumers and homes of the multinationals, there was a history of unseemly behaviour and jockeying for position. In particular, the British government made strenuous efforts to keep United States interests out of the Middle East. In this it was successful until 1930 when BAPCO obtained a concession in Bahrain and later the ARAMCO Group were awarded a concession covering the entire territory of Saudi Arabia.

The effects of this long period of latter-day colonialism and Byzantine intrigue are still felt in the region today. The word 'concession' is highly emotive, recording the establishment of such very one-sided partnerships.

Much of the residual anti-Western feeling in the region, which has given rise occasionally to demagogues, stems from the period when producer countries fought to free themselves from the iron embrace of the international oil corporations.

Although the exact terms of agreement varied from country to country, the concessions were generally large and all-embracing. In the cases of Kuwait, Qatar and Bahrain, they included the entire country. The duration specified was usually up to seventy-five years and the privileges included the exclusive rights to control all aspects of the oil and related products industries from the initial prospecting to the export of refined products. Furthermore, within the producer countries, the corporations enjoyed a wide range of rights and privileges which rendered them free from local government control. A United Nations report, *Review of Economic Conditions in the Middle East* (1951) summarized the position as follows:

> The terms of their concessions give the foreign companies a freedom of action which substantially insulates them from the economy of Middle Eastern countries . . . hence, the impact of oil operations in Middle Eastern producer countries is mainly indirect and the benefits derived from them are limited.

The injustices were so obvious that, on attaining their independence, the oil producers increasingly demanded renegotiation. From the beginning of the Second World War until the foundation of OPEC in 1960, the power of the multinationals and their home governments was gradually curtailed as a result either of negotiations or of nationalization. However, the road was far from smooth. The acquisition of full control was begun by Iran, with the nationalization of the Anglo-Iranian Oil Companies Concession in 1951. Despite the fact that Britain was at the time in the throes of nationalizing its own industries, the British government, together with the oil Majors, declared what was effectively an embargo on Iranian oil. As a result, the Iranian Premier, Mohammed Mossadeq, who had been mainly instrumental in the passage of the Oil Nationalization Act (1953) was deposed before an accommodation was reached in 1954. The outcome was that the Shah repealed the Act, but the principle of nationalization remained. There was an agreed 50/50 share-out between the new consortium, consisting of British and American interest and the Iranian government. That settlement broke the log-jam and from then on there were successful moves to reduce the areal scale and duration of concessions and to increase the share of the profits enjoyed by the consumer countries. Furthermore, as indicated earlier, the entry of the Independents into the market produced a further amelioration of conditions. Whereas the earlier concessions in Iran and Iraq had involved thousands of square kilometres for half a century or more, by 1970 the average concession was limited to a few hundred square kilometres for a period of about ten years.

The new system was seen in operation in the case of Libya, which was determined that its oil should not be monopolized by the Majors. The concessions, comprising fifty-one separate areas, were awarded to seventeen oil-producing companies, many of them comparatively small. Further, the concessions were granted for relatively short periods and, if undeveloped, had to be returned to the government. The role of the corporations was being forcibly changed from that of a concessionaire to that of a contractor.

All these moves towards a fairer return on resources for the producer countries were given an impetus by the creation of OPEC in 1960. Although the cartel met with only limited initial success, its formation formalized the key change in the pattern of relationships. From a position of virtual corporation monopoly, the producer countries had gradually negotiated and legislated their way towards a more equitable position. The establishment of OPEC finally signalled that economic independence was to be congruent with political independence and the producers were to control their own destinies.

The instigator of moves towards cooperation between producers and confrontation with the corporations had been not a Middle Eastern country, but Venezuela. Following initial contacts, a Venezuelan delegation was sent to the Middle East in 1949 and this was followed by the signing of a Saudi Arabia–Iraq agreement in 1953. However, the trigger factor, responsible for the creation of OPEC, was the dissatisfaction within the producer countries over price reductions made by the Majors in 1959 and 1960. This action reduced at a stroke the posted prices of Middle Eastern oil to a level below that of 1953. The five key exporting countries, Saudi Arabia, Iraq, Iran, Kuwait and Venezuela, met in Baghdad in August 1960 and on 15 September the Organization of Petroleum Exporting Countries (OPEC) was announced. The main aims were to press for the restoration of prices and to develop a stable pricing policy. OPEC was to coordinate the export policies of the member states and thereby guarantee themselves a stable income. Three of the original founder members were Arab states and their moves towards a fuller economic intregration led to the formation in 1968 of the Organization of Arab Petroleum Exporting Countries (OAPEC).

The initial impact of OPEC was very limited and the 1967 Arab–Israeli war merely exposed the lack of cooperation. In retaliation for their support for Israel, the Arab countries placed an embargo on supplies to several Western consumers. However, the effect was nullified when non-OPEC Arab members simply increased their production. On the other hand, one effect of the war did have lasting consequences. The closure of the Suez Canal altered the pattern of trade routes, introduced new vulnerabilities for the consumer countries, and increased costs. This new situation benefited Nigeria and Libya, both far closer to the main markets of Western Europe and North America. When the civil war in Nigeria disrupted oil production, Libya was left in the most favourable position. Following the overthrow of the monarchy in September 1969, the new regime promptly capitalized on the position by increasing prices. At first, the Libyan move was opposed, but when cut-backs in production were implemented and the Western oil situation became more serious, the new prices were accepted. This initiative provided the lead and, following meetings in Tehran and Tripoli in 1971, both prices and the tax rate on profits were increased.

Throughout the post-war period up until this time, the price of oil in real terms had remained generally stable and had, at times, declined. Indeed, many experts consider that the major price rise of some 70 per cent which OPEC imposed during the Arab–Israeli war of 1973 did less than restore the position. However, with cutbacks in production and further world shortages, the OPEC members were able to raise the price again in late 1973 by 128 per cent. The price then stood at $11.65 per barrel, hardly excessive in the light of the vast profits which the corporations had been making.

The new prices had a number of effects, some beneficial, others less so. Most importantly perhaps, Arab pride, which had been so dented during the earlier years of the century, was restored. Vast fortunes were made within the producing countries, to which there was a massive transfer of wealth. With their low absorptive capacities, the influx of petro-dollars could not be directly accommodated and the very large surplus was invested in Western banks. Thus, not only did the Middle Eastern countries control the oil, but they were also extremely influential in the world banking system and, indeed, in the fiscal affairs of many Western countries. This represented, therefore, a complete reversal of fortune. On the debit side, while the newly acquired wealth led to improved conditions, it also resulted in excesses.

The effects on consumers were equally dramatic as price rises were felt at petrol pumps. For the first time, the West became aware of the profligate way in which it had been using an exhaustible resource. Conservation measures were seriously studied and implemented. Also, exploration efforts increased and new sources of oil were gradually brought onstream.

Relative price stability ensued until 1978–9 when Iranian oil production was suspended, following the Revolution. Prices were raised in stages until, in early 1980, they peaked at over $43 per barrel. At that stage, prices had risen by $40 per barrel in a decade. This time, however, the effect world-wide was less dramatic in that production could be increased from a range of new sources, while the conservation methods enacted in the early 1970s were by now bearing fruit. Thus, during the 1980s, prices fluctuated and generally fell back, particularly during 1986, when OPEC introduced netback pricing. The oil-rich countries of the Middle East, as a result, found their economies on the wrong growth curve and, despite earnings from overseas investments, there were cut-backs in development. The situation was exacerbated by the fact that this was a totally new situation for the governments. In most cases, since their independence, the main problems had concerned the distribution of an increasing wealth. Suddenly, as resources became scarcer, priorities had to be established and a system of allocation implemented.

Prices recovered towards the end of the decade, but never again approached the peak achieved in 1980. Likewise, the production figure for 1979 remains the highest achieved in the Persian/Arabian Gulf and the Middle East as a whole. The geopolitical changes of 1989 resulted in a slight upward trend in prices and by August 1990 a barrel fetched $18. The onset of the present crisis, however, unleashed a flurry of activity in the oil industry and prices briefly broke the $40 per barrel barrier during late September 1990. According to Sheikh Ahmad Yamani, Oil Minister for Saudi Arabia from 1962 to 1966, the present price rise indicates yet another change in the oil power game. According to his reasoning (*The Independent on*

Sunday, 14 October 1990), the changes attendant upon the price rises of 1973–4, reflecting the split in power between OPEC and the major corporations, resulted in a dispersion of that power and the entry on to the scene of other players. Increasingly, the price of oil was to be set, not by insiders, but in the Rotterdam market. This spot market allowed shortfalls and surpluses to be accommodated and the definition of the price of oil became the price at which these marginal barrels changed hands. The importance can be seen from the fact that both OPEC and the oil corporations began pegging their contracts to the spot market. Thus, with the Iranian Revolution in 1979 and the sudden disappearance of Iranian production, surplus oil was rapidly purchased and the spot price rocketed. According to Yamani, this was the first time that oil prices had been driven by psychology. During the conservative mid-1980s, the corporations came to rely even more upon the spot market and they effectively surrendered control of the oil prices at the margin. Thus, it was open to risk managers and a new category of oil man emerged: the Wall Street refiner. The consequent introduction of options and futures markets brought new volatility to oil prices. The price of oil was thereby redefined as that quoted in the futures market rather than that traded at the present time. Thus, to quote Yamani:

> By the end of the 1980s, as a result, the oil world bore little resemblance to the world the public imagined it to be. It was no longer dominated by big companies and OPEC, but by a trading system sharing out risk and reward in a manner few lay people understand.

Thus, on 2 August 1990, when Iraq invaded Kuwait, oil prices increased rapidly, not as a result of shortage, nor of hoarding, but of psychology. Further, this was the kind of psychology from which the new breed of oil men benefited. Volatility is in their life-blood and they have learned to live with it.

Thus, in many ways, the wheel has turned full circle. Power is once again being exercised by those operating far from the oilfields. While they may lack the manipulative opportunities of the Majors, their interests do not coincide with those of the Middle Eastern countries. The Middle East requires political stability and also stable oil prices.

The present position

The pre-eminence of the Middle East in oil resources is clear (Figure 4.1). Excluding those of the Soviet Union, there are twelve mega-fields (those with reserves over 1,000 million barrels) in the world, all of them in the Middle East (Table 4.1). Iran has five, Iraq two, Kuwait one, Saudi Arabia three and Libya one. The two largest, four to five times bigger than the average are Ghawar in Saudi Arabia, followed by Burgan in Kuwait.

It is considered by most oil experts that there are no mega-oilfields yet to be discovered. The relative importance of Middle Eastern oil can be assessed from various issues of the annual *BP Statistical Review of World Energy.* In 1979, Middle Eastern oil output peaked when it produced 39 per cent of the world's supply. During the 1980s, the figure fluctuated, reaching

Table 4.1 The twelve mega-fields of the Middle East

Location	Year of discovery
Iran	
Agha Jari	1938
Gach Saran	1928
Marun	1964
Bibi Hakimeh	1961
Ahwaz	1958
Iraq	
Kirkuk	1929
Rumaila	1953
Kuwait	
Burgan	1931
Saudi Arabia	
Ghawar	1948
Safaniya	1951
Abqaiq	1940
Libya	
Sarir	1961

a low of 24 per cent in 1985. By 1989, the Middle East was producing 31 per cent of the world's oil. However, more important than production is potential and this is shown by proved reserves. Proved reserves of oil are generally taken to be those quantities which geological and engineering information indicates, with reasonable certainty, can be recovered in the future from known reservoirs, under existing operating and economic conditions (*BP Statistical Review of World Energy*, 1990). However, such statistics still need to be treated with caution since proved reserves in the Middle East have increased by a factor of at least 12 since 1950. For example, there was a major reappraisal in 1987 involving four countries: Iran, Iraq, the United Arab Emirates (Abu Dhabi) and Venezuela. The result of this revision was that world proved reserves had increased by some 27 per cent. In the cases of Iran, which reported an increase of 90 per cent, and Iraq, 112 per cent, some scepticism has been expressed, particularly since at that time those two countries were locked in what seemed to be an interminable war. It was pointed out in the *Oil and Gas Journal* (27 November 1987) that the figures might be related to government expectation that production quotas within OPEC were to be allocated on the basis of proved reserves. On the other hand, during 1987, there was an upturn in prices and this, in theory, should lead to increased reserves since further exploration and enhanced extraction should result.

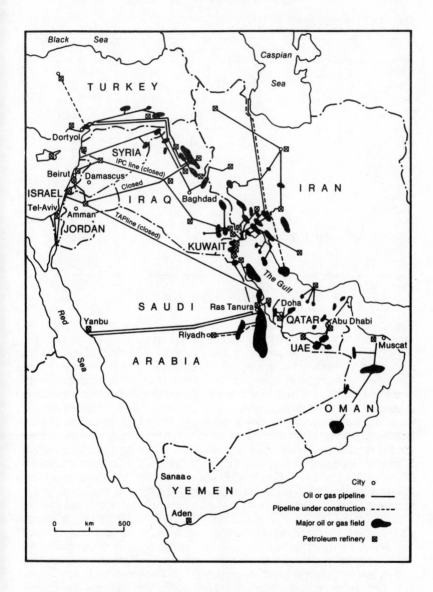

Figure 4.1 The petroleum industry in the region

Table 4.2 illustrates the dominance of the Persian/Arabian Gulf with respect to proved reserves. While the Gulf has almost two-thirds of the currently assessed reserves, Saudi Arabia, alone, has over a quarter. As reserves within the Western World in general and the United States and

Table 4.2 Proved oil reserves, 1989

	% world	R/P ratio
USA	3.4	10:0
USSR	5.8	13:1
Persian/Arabian Gulf	65.2	*
(S. Arabia	25.2	*)
Mexico	5.6	55:7
Venezuela	5.8	84:7
Nigeria	1.6	27:5
Libya	2.3	54:9
Algeria	0.9	23:7
People's Republic of China	2.3	22:8
Norway	1.1	20:2

* over 100 years
[S. Arabia in parenthesis is subsumed in Persian/Arabian Gulf]

Soviet Union in particular decline, the only other sources presently available are those shown. Mexico and Venezuela have comparatively large reserves, but both are higher-debtor developing countries. Similarly, Nigeria with sizeable reserves will require increasing amounts for its own development. Therefore, among these three, there is likely to be little surplus. Next in order are Libya and China, both of which present strategic risks. At present, Libyan oil is banned in the United States. The only other countries with over 0.9 per cent of proved reserves are Norway and Algeria. Thus, as oil conditions become tighter towards the end of this century, options outside the Persian/Arabian Gulf for obtaining oil are very restricted. This view is reinforced by the reserves to production (R/P) ratio. This is defined in the *BP Statistical View of World Energy* (1990): if the reserves remaining at the end of any year are divided by the production of that year, the result is the remaining length of time that those reserves would last if production were to continue at the then current level. Since the ratio depends not only upon proved reserves, but upon production rates, which are dependent upon economic and geological factors, it is a rather less accurate guide. As reserves decline, there are likely to be strong moves towards conservation and strenuous efforts to improve the proportion extracted.

If figures for producers within the Gulf region are examined, the reappraisals by Iran and Iraq have resulted in the relative downgrading of Kuwait, which, until 1987, was clearly the second most important country in the world. Table 4.3 shows that the Emirate of Abu Dhabi, Iran, Iraq and Kuwait all have similar proved reserves, but all lag well behind Saudi Arabia. The table also shows the three countries whose reserves will last well over 100 years.

Table 4.3 Proved oil reserves: Persian/Arabian Gulf, 1989

	% world	R/P ratio
Abu Dhabi	9.1	*
Dubai	0.4	34:4
Iran	9.2	89:1
Iraq	9.9	97:0
Kuwait	9.3	*
Neutral Zone	0.5	35:5
Oman	0.4	20:1
Qatar	0.4	31:5
Saudi Arabia	25.2	*

*over 100 years

During the 1980s, oil production in the Persian/Arabian Gulf has been reduced as demand has declined, although the 1989 figure is the highest since 1980. Ever since, there has been a gradual annual rise. The overall decline, particularly evident in the mid-1980s, resulted in a general world slump in economic growth rates, improved conservation procedures, output from new suppliers, and the effects of some substitution, particularly in Western Europe and Japan. While production in both the United States and the Soviet Union has continued to decline, that of the Persian/Arabian Gulf shows a 10 per cent increase over the past twelve months (Table 4.4.).

Table 4.4 World oil production, 1989

	m. tonnes	% share of world	% change from 1988
USA	433.8	14.0	− 6.3
USSR	607.5	19.7	− 2.6
Persian/Arabian Gulf	814.0	26.3	+10.3
Mexico	141.2	4.6	+ 0.2
Venezuela	99.2	3.2	+ 3.1
Libya	54.8	1.6	+ 7.0
Nigeria	79.1	2.6	+17.0
Algeria	50.4	1.6	+ 7.0
People's Republic of China	138.3	4.5	+ 0.9

Within the Persian/Arabian Gulf region, the predominance of Saudi Arabia is again clear, as are the important contributions of Iran, Iraq, Kuwait and the Emirate of Abu Dhabi. However, of more interest are the percentage changes over the past twelve months (Table 4.5). These indicate that despite the relatively depressed price, Iran, Abu Dhabi and Kuwait have greatly

Table 4.5 Oil production: Persian/Arabian Gulf, 1989

	m. tonnes	% share of world	% change from 1988
Abu Dhabi	75.4	2.4	+25.3
Dubai	23.2	0.7	− 4.5
Iran	142.2	4.6	+26.0
Iraq	138.6	4.5	+ 8.5
Kuwait	79.4	2.6	+19.0
Oman	29.4	0.9	− 1.5
Qatar	18.7	0.6	+10.6
Saudi Arabia	256.5	8.3	− 0.3

increased their production. Oil consumption has remained comparatively steady, with a minor decline in both the United States and the Soviet Union. However, the main point illustrated by Table 4.6 is that the United States is still using over one-quarter of the world's oil and Western Europe almost one-fifth.

Table 4.6 Oil consumption, 1989

	m. tonnes	% world	% change from 1988
USA	792.6	25.6	−0.1
USSR	434.7	14.0	−1.0
Persian/Arabian Gulf	140.3	4.5	+3.8
W Europe	591.7	19.1	−0.4
Japan	232.8	7.5	−3.6
People's Republic of China	117.1	3.8	+6.3

If the figures for reserves, production and consumption as world percentages are examined, it can be seen that the United States has an adverse reserves to production ratio and a marked import dependence. In the case of Western Europe, the situation is even more extreme. However, as would be expected, the opposite obtains for the Persian/Arabian Gulf (Table 4.7).

Table 4.7 Key statistics (% of world), 1989

	Reserves	Production	Consumption
USA	3.4	14.0	25.6
USSR	5.8	19.7	14.0
Persian/Arabian Gulf	65.2	26.3	4.5
W. Europe	1.8	6.2	19.1

In summary, these tables all illustrate clearly the vital importance of Persian/Arabian Gulf oil for the world economy at the present time and for the future. It might be considered that some relief could be found in the use of natural gas, an increasingly important element in world trade. However, if the statistics for natural gas reserves are examined (Table 4.8), it can be seen that with the major exception of the Soviet Union and, to a much lesser extent, the United States, the Middle East again predominates. With current rates of production, the most assured supplies are all in the Persian/Arabian Gulf, being located in Iran, the Emirate of Abu Dhabi, Saudi Arabia, Qatar and Iraq. The only non-Middle Eastern countries, apart from the superpowers, with more than 2 per cent of the world reserves are Canada, Indonesia and Norway.

Table 4.8 Proved natural gas reserves, 1989

	% world	R/P ratio
USSR	37.6	53:2
Iran	12.5	*
USA	4.1	9:6
Abu Dhabi	4.6	*
Qatar	4.1	*
Saudi Arabia	4.5	*
Algeria	2.9	72:3
Norway	2.1	72:8
Iraq	2.4	*
Indonesia	2.2	62:0
Canada	2.4	27:2

*over 100 years

The other main alternative to oil has long been deemed to be nuclear energy. The long-term scenario has been that as oil declines during the early part of next century, so nuclear power will plug the gap before developments allow the general use of solar power. This thinking has subsequently been modified in the light of safety problems and public antagonism. These have dictated in all the industrialized countries except France a slow uptake of nuclear energy. Table 4.9 shows the comparatively low nuclear to oil percentage use for all the countries, except France and, to a lesser extent, West Germany. It can be seen that attempts to overcome dependence upon Middle Eastern oil and particularly the use of Persian/Arabian Gulf oil through the use of substitutes are fraught with problems. Furthermore, there are many uses for which there are no substitutes and apparently none towards which scientific research is advancing. Therefore,

Table 4.9 Nuclear energy consumption, 1989

	m. tonnes oil equivalent	nuclear:oil %
USA	142.2	18
USSR	45.4	10
France	59.9	68
UK	15.0	17
W. Germany	33.1	31
Japan	46.3	20

it must be concluded that oil will maintain its pivotal role in world energy supplies for the foreseeable future and that the Persian/Arabian Gulf will remain the key global geopolitical flashpoint. Geopolitical vulnerability is heightened when the sea-lanes are taken into consideration. Tables of imports (*BP Statistical Review of World Energy*, 1990) show that, with the exception of the United States, all of the major regions of the world receive the bulk of their imports from the Persian/Arabian Gulf. The most significant figures are: the United States 24 per cent, Western Europe 42 per cent, Asia (excluding China and Japan) 76 per cent, and Japan 67 per cent. The Persian/ Arabian Gulf is responsible for 42 per cent of world trade in oil, the next highest statistics being those for the Soviet Union (13 per cent) and Latin America (11 per cent).

Oil and development

For all the countries around the littoral of the Persian/Arabian Gulf, petroleum products account for 85 per cent or more of export earnings. The lowest figure is 85 per cent for Bahrain, the most diversified economy within the region. The highest is over 95 per cent for Iraq and Oman. Therefore, for all of these countries oil is closely identified with development. This is a mixed blessing. The volatility of the oil market, indicated earlier, has of course directly affected revenues accruing to the producing countries and has produced major economic difficulties. In general terms, the decade of the 1970s was one of surplus, while that of the 1980s was one of deficit. The high hopes and expectations engendered from the mid-1970s onwards was gradually dissipated by the mid-1980s. The revenue pattern of Saudi Arabia provides an illustration of the problem. During the early 1970s, oil revenues rose only slowly to some $2 billion in 1973. Following the 1973–4 price rise, they leapt almost immediately to $20 billion in 1974. The figure continued to increase gradually until early 1979 when the next price 'shock' produced a revenue in 1981 of $100 billion. Revenues fell sharply from that peak, levelled temporarily during 1982, then plummeted, so that by 1985 the total earned was only $30 billion.

In *The Closed Circle*, David Pryce-Jones[3] provides many illustrations of the effects of these sudden and vast increases in wealth upon Arab society during the oil years. As a whole, the Arab countries exported oil worth over $1,200 billion and from the proceeds more than $600 billion was used to import a wide range of Western commodities and consumer goods and, most significantly, arms: 'Even Mecca . . . has been overwhelmed by clover leaves and over-passes, by tall office buildings, supermarkets, parking garages and deluxe hotels . . .' The rate of change, frequently euphemistically labelled 'progress' by national leaders, was breathtaking. Many passed from a camel to a Mercedes in one generation and the different societies, in general, could not absorb the changes. Depending upon the stratum of society, the result was reflected in excesses of materialism, religion and nationalism.

Nonetheless, despite the often apparent abuses, solid economic development did take place. Transport infrastructures were improved, urban amenities were installed and large amounts were spent on the social services and education. Dwellings of mud-brick were replaced by villas and even marble palaces, dirt tracks were converted to first-class highways, and international airports proliferated. However, even in all of this there was an element of excess. In the United Arab Emirates, there are now three competing international airports within a few kilometres of each other. In many parts of the Gulf there are now surplus hospital and university places, while agriculture and heavy industry have often burgeoned on the back of vast subsidies. The government of Saudi Arabia has been offering wheat-growers a procurement price which is at least seven times the current world commercial price.

The leaner years of the 1980s have reduced the level of government spending, forcing cut-backs in development projects and depressing business activity. There has been a positive feedback effect, illustrated by Shireen Hunter in her article, 'The Gulf Economic Crisis and its Social and Political Consequences':[4] 'These developments have induced an exodus of immigrant workers which, by reducing economic demand, rents and real estate values, has further depressed business.'

The other key factor was the Iran–Iraq war and the support given by many of the Gulf Cooperation Council states to Iraq. This led to a further drain on resources and an economic recession which put at risk the financial and banking systems.

As economic expectations were not fulfilled, so social divisions were exacerbated. Social mobility was reduced as employment opportunities for the newly educated declined. Ethnic and religious differences, submerged in the general prosperity, suddenly re-emerged. Dissatisfaction was fuelled by the overall belief that governments had failed. The question posed remains unanswered: why, after the huge revenue receipts of the oil years, are the Gulf economies still vulnerable to the volatility of the international oil market?

It is undoubtedly too early to assess the overall effects of the last two decades on the economies of the Persian/Arabian Gulf oil producers. Nonetheless, certain pointers are available. Technically, it was accepted wisdom that development in the burgeoning countries was constrained by unfavourable terms of trade, which limited growth in the primary commodity sector, and by the modest amounts of capital and foreign exchange available. In the 1970s, the Gulf countries enjoyed favourable terms of trade, together with vast inputs of capital and foreign exchange. Why have they therefore not developed further and reached some kind of take-off? The oil sector has been used as a growth pole, but development has been mismanaged and generally narrowly focused. With vast wealth available, the norms of economic discipline, such as they are, could be disregarded. In the general euphoria provided by vast revenues, misjudgements could pass unnoticed and misguided policies could be pursued beyond the point of no return. Thus, many commentators have seen certain advantages in the present, more straitened circumstances. Economic disciplines have to be imposed and more lasting all-round developments may be achieved. Nonetheless, it must be concluded that the oil boom, both in its upturn and in its downturn, has resulted in massive disruption.

Such disruption is well illustrated in the rural areas of many of the Gulf states. Oil revenues led to massive urban expansion and the rural population provided a ready source of cheap labour. Skilled and experienced rural craftsmen and agriculturalists became unskilled and, lately, unemployed urban and industrial workers. As men with initiative left the villages, so enterprise died with those they left behind. Nevertheless, rural labour was in increasingly short supply and higher rewards could be demanded. These were provided initially by remittances from the itinerant urban workforce. Money received tended to be spent on imported goods, so that Western products replaced home crafts. One result of this was the demise of the craft industries, which meant that the old and disabled were unable to contribute to village life. Thus, the rural community became increasingly obsolete and irrelevant. This situation was reinforced by the increasing range of activities such as education and health care taken up by the government. Lack of planning and forethought can also be illustrated in the much-vaunted heavy industrial sector. From the mid-1970s, the countries of the Persian/Arabian Gulf began to develop their own petrochemical industries in an attempt to broaden their industrial bases and to enhance the profits made from their primary product. Furthermore, they had surplus revenue for the exercise, the price of oil compared with that in Europe to Western competitors was highly favourable, there was an opportunity to use rather than waste their natural gas, and there were optimistic forecasts about world agriculture and the requirement for fertilizers. Finally, many of the major oil companies were keen to cooperate in joint ventures. As a result, major complexes were established in Qatar, Saudi Arabia, Kuwait, Iraq, the UAE and Oman. Between 1977 and 1985, production of both ammonia and urea tripled in the region.

However, the petrochemical boom of the late 1960s was followed by a notable decline in the late 1970s. For a variety of reasons, the world economy had gone into recession and the result was over-capacity. But this was only one problem. Fundamentally, the development of a petrochemical industry in an environment such as that of the Gulf was a very high-cost endeavour. Equipment needed to be imported, construction times were longer and in many cases there was no pre-existing infrastructure. There was also a shortage of skilled labour and technical staff and, surprisingly, frequently of feed stock. Much of the natural gas is associated with oil and with cut-backs in oil production there was less gas available. Furthermore, as the industry had moved downstream, so it met the full force of competition from the West. By producing more sophisticated products, it cut itself off from many of the more obvious Third World outlets. Despite the growth of cooperation through bodies such as the GCC, there was no coordination in the development of the petrochemical or indeed the other heavy industries. As a result, essentially unviable industries were competing with each other within the Gulf.

It can be concluded that oil has provided development opportunities but as yet the potential has not been realized. Oil will continue to be vital to the West and therefore Western manipulation is likely to remain a factor of life. Within the Persian/Arabian Gulf itself, it is only possible to express ambivalence about the benefits of oil. Thus, dependence upon oil seems guaranteed to enhance the already wide range of cleavages apparent in the societies of the Gulf producer countries.

Notes

1. p. 177 Times Books, New York, 1990.
2. Mana Saeed al-Otaiba, *OPEC and the Petroleum Industry*, p. 25, John Wiley and Sons, New York, 1975.
3. Pryce-Jones, D. *The Closed Circle*, pp. 265–66, Paladin, London.
4. *Middle East Journal*, Vol. 40, No. 4, 1986.

Chapter 5
Potential crisis factors

For many compelling reasons, the Middle East, and particularly the Persian/
Arabian Gulf, has long occupied the centre of world attention and has been
designated the crucial geopolitical flashpoint. Among the major factors
contributing to its importance are that:

(a) it has been the crossroads of the world since ancient times;
(b) it is the chief repository of a key modern commodity;
(c) it represents the greatest focus of Western dependence;
(d) it is the region which has witnessed the greatest transfer of wealth in
     history.

Given that background, it is hardly surprising that there have been recurrent
crises in the area. What of the future? The development of the major crisis
components — Islamic fundamentalism, Arab nationalism and oil — has
already been traced and their contributions to the Iraq–Kuwait crisis
identified. Whatever the future may hold, it seems most unlikely that this will
be the last crisis. Indeed, no less a figure than Winston Churchill himself, as
First Lord of the Admiralty, predicted that the last great clash would occur
in the Middle East, the final scene being acted on the plain of Armageddon.
There is, as yet, little evidence to dismiss so apocalyptic a vision.

The range of potential crisis factors is wide, but they can be grouped
according to the scale of their likely effect. The major crisis factor with
world-wide repercussions is oil, particularly in the context of the security of
superpowers and the most important industrialized nations. Factors more
likely to be restricted to regional importance include the overspill from
current conflicts — although in the case of the Arab–Israeli dispute this quite
clearly has global overtones — the effects of fundamentalism and
nationalism, the influence of differing ideologies, hydropolitics and
boundary disputes. Problems posed by expatriates, the effects of
modernization and education, the potential clash over religious beliefs and
problems resulting from the rigid internal structure, are all potential crisis
factors and likely to be operative on a national scale.

The oil weapon

The idea of the oil weapon implies the geopolitical use of oil. In other words, what is normally considered to be the commercial transaction of a key commodity is distorted for purely political purposes. In the case of the Persian/Arabian Gulf states, they can exert oil power as a result of the laws of supply and demand. Oil is strategic in that it is a vital resource for modern life, most developed countries are dependent upon imports, and the number of possible sources is limited. As shown earlier, given the present reserves to production ratio, the major producers during the early part of next century will be limited almost exclusively to the Gulf. In effect, the Gulf states are moving increasingly towards a monopoly position and as a result cartels such as OPEC are likely to be more and more effective.

This position of geopolitical advantage has produced dissension within and among the Gulf states. In essence, the question is: should oil be produced at the rates required by Western economies or the rates most favourable for the producer states? If output were cut, prices would rise and the untapped reserves would increase in value. Libya carried out such a policy, but only for a specific purpose and over a very limited time. After the end of its war with Iran, Iraq also urged cut-backs so that prices could be pushed up from approximately $12 to $18 per barrel. Its reconstruction programme was drawn up on the basis of such a price. Furthermore, as the price per barrel declines, so more oil needs to be pumped to obtain the same revenues.

That producers have been, in general, unwilling to damage Western interests by restricting the oil flow can be explained in a number of ways. The Gulf states are heavily dependent upon the Western food market and the threat of food geopolitics was made by Henry Kissinger in 1973. Western technology is also important, but in most cases, with both food and technology, other sources might be found. Perhaps the most important factor is that the producers have invested heavily in the West and therefore its solvency is important in protecting their assets. Finally, of course, there is the military question and the somewhat ambiguous statements which have sometimes emanated from the West. Ultimately, as illustrated in the Iraq–Kuwait crisis, the oil states of the Arabian Peninsula are dependent upon the West for their security. As alternative oil supplies decline, so the security of the major producers within the Persian/Arabian Gulf region will become an even greater priority. The question then might be how the West would regard unilateral action, such as a deliberate reduction in output.

In his State of the Union Speech in January 1980, President Jimmy Carter stated that the United States would be prepared to use force if necessary, to protect its vital interests in the Persian Gulf. The immediate result was the formation of the Rapid Deployment Force, later known as the Rapid Deployment Joint Task Force and now as the Central Command. Agreed access was negotiated on the Indian Ocean atoll of Diego Garcia and to facilities, basically air bases, in Oman, Somalia, Kenya and Egypt. Initially, the 'Carter doctrine', as it was known, was aimed specifically at the Soviet Union, but later the mission of the Rapid Deployment Force was expanded to include both regional and domestic contingencies. This latter development provided such freedom of action that it caused grave disquiet among even Western-orientated Gulf states. The conditions under which the United States would move to protect its vital interests had never been clarified. In the case of the Iraq–Kuwait crisis, the massive military build-up resulted from some sort of invitation from King Fahd, although it was admitted within the US administration that Saudi Arabia was not in danger of attack.

That America's vital interests are at risk if Persian/Arabian Gulf supplies are disrupted should not be doubted. It was shown clearly by Henry Rowen in a recent Brookings publication, *Oil and American Security,*[1] that the overall GNP loss in the United States from the interruptions which actually occurred in 1973–4 and in 1979–80 were 5 per cent and 3 per cent respectively. Even if the United States were completely independent of Gulf oil, there would be a substantial GNP loss as a result of the world-wide economic dislocation, attendant upon supply disruption. As was illustrated in 1973–4, the military would also be severely affected. Although the overall shortfall was only some 7 per cent, the West broke up in disarray and many countries, neglecting previous assurances of solidarity, negotiated bilateral agreements with oil-producing states. OPEC members reduced supplies and introduced an embargo on oil shipments to the United States, the Netherlands and Canada. Such was the prevalent anxiety that several key NATO countries denied landing and over-flying rights to US aircraft. At the same time, shortages compelled the US Navy to reduce ship time at sea by 20 per cent and the Air Force to reduce flying time by some 33 per cent. Indeed, by the end of 1973, there is clear evidence, discussed by Ian Lesser in Resources and Strategy,[2] that NATO operations were constrained. Thus, although the restrictions were comparatively minor and short-lived, the effect on operational capabilities was immediate.

From an examination of the effects of relatively modest fluctuations in supply, it is concluded that oil constitutes a potent weapon. The countries of the Persian/Arabian Gulf can exercise global political influence as a result of their oil and their understanding of this fact allows them to exert effective leverage.

The superpowers

Until November 1989, the world was viewed geopolitically in a bipolar context. The claims of China, following the *rapprochement* with the United States after the visit of President Nixon in 1972, to be a third pole are still not universally accepted. With the moves towards EC 1992 and the obvious economic power of Japan, it can be safely concluded that the world from the early 1990s will be multipolar. However, at present, the two great powers capable of exercising real influence in the Gulf remain the United States and the Soviet Union. The Soviet Union is a military superpower and, whatever the effects of arms limitation agreements, can, unless destabilized from within, continue to pose a threat to the Middle East and particularly the Persian/Arabian Gulf.

Until 15 February 1989, when it officially withdrew, the Soviet Union was perceived, by the West at least, to threaten stability in the region by its occupation of Afghanistan. The reason for its first use of troops outside the Eastern Bloc has been hotly disputed. Some experts saw it as merely a move to prevent the destabilization of a contiguous friendly state; others, mindful of the 50 million Muslims who inhabit the southern central states of the Soviet Union, considered that it was designed to prevent fundamentalist contamination. Given the regimes already established in Ethiopia and South Yemen, some saw it as a pincer movement to surround the Gulf and cut off Chinese influence. Yet more involved scenarios foresaw the establishment of a platform in Afghanistan from which Baluchistan could be destabilized and strategic points along the Makran coast established. Whatever the original intent, and it was probably a combination of circumstances which resulted in the Soviet advance, certain outcomes are now clear. The involvement in Afghanistan gave the Soviet Union a platform, either on the edge of or actually in the Middle East, according to definition. During almost a decade of occupation, the infrastructure was vastly improved and therefore any such advance could be repeated far more rapidly if required. Finally and most importantly, the government in Kabul is now reasonably stable. Najibullah has altered the structure and approach of his government so that it would not be characterized as secular, rather than Marxist. The mujahedin have, despite the prophecies of most Western experts, been singularly unsuccessful since the Soviet withdrawal. Apart from the fragmentation within the movement, the most obvious explanation of this must be that local people are reasonably satisfied with the Najibullah government. Indeed, such is the apparent accepted legitimacy of the government that, as reported in The Guardian (22 November 1990), meetings between the government and certain mujahedin leaders have already taken place. It should also perhaps be remembered that, in the manner understood in the Western World, Afghanistan has never been a unified state. Rather, it has comprised a series of fiefdoms, many with loyalties which straddle the international borders. Thus, it may be that Afghanistan is about to enter into a state of unification not previously enjoyed. Whatever happens, it seems very likely that relations with the Soviet Union will remain comparatively strong. Therefore, the fear of a spill-over from the war into the Middle East has now been dispelled, but the Soviet Union has been enabled to retain its geopolitical position in Middle Eastern affairs.

The 'fundamentalist curtain'

Before the rapprochement between the superpowers, the West had devoted a great deal of effort in attempting to confine the influence of the Soviet Union. The basic tenets developed by Sir Halford Mackinder and, later, Nicholas Spykman, still very largely influenced strategic thinking. According to their ideas, it was imperative that no one power controlled the 'World Island' or the 'Rimland' and therefore great emphasis was placed upon attempting to develop treaties among the 'Rimland' states. Further, it was felt that should one of the 'Rimland' states succumb to communism, there would be a 'domino' effect, which would result in the collapse of all its neighbours. Thus, a series of treaties, inspired largely by the United States and the United Kingdom, was enacted to provide boundary blocs in key world positions. The main examples were NATO, CENTO (originally the Baghdad Pact) and SEATO. However, while NATO and SEATO survived in modified form, CENTO eventually collapsed. The gateway to the Middle East was thus left open.

Conspiracy theory asserts that the West then developed a rather long, drawn-out plan to constrain any advances by the Soviet Union. Towards the end of the 1960s, the Ayatollah Khomeini was gradually developing his network of mullahs and propounding his ideas of fundamentalism. The Shah of Iran, the strong man of the region, eventually recognized the potential for subversion in what was being propagated and Khomeini was exiled to Iraq. However, he was still able to continue building his political structure. That he was not eliminated by the Shah's regime may be attributed to the power of religion, but more possibly it stemmed from the fact that other key events were occurring in the Gulf. In particular, the withdrawal of UK forces in the first years of the 1970s left Iran as the key pillar of the 'twin pillar' policy of the United States which had taken over effective leadership in the region. Furthermore, the oil price rises of 1973–4 had furnished Iran with greatly increased revenues. Thus, the country was without doubt the regional superpower. The other pillar, Saudi Arabia, possessed revenues on a grand scale, but it had a tiny population and no effective military presence.

Later, when the danger of Khomeini was comprehended more fully, he was exiled to Paris, but he was still permitted to broadcast subversive propaganda to followers in Iran. Again, the question must be asked as to why this was allowed to happen and why he himself was not removed by one of the many state bodies capable of perpetrating such an act. Since his purpose was so obvious, the explanation has been advanced that the United States was already losing faith in the Shah's regime which was becoming increasingly unpopular and more corrupt. As a result, it urged restraint and preserved Khomeini in the mistaken view that any regime he might establish would be benign and pro-Western. Certainly, it seems reasonable to consider that would-be state assassins were restrained.

The ideal result of a Khomeini regime would be a fundamentalist 'curtain', fulfilling more effectively the role once undertaken by CENTO. With 50 million Muslim citizens in its south-central states, any Soviet moves beyond its borders in the region would be likely to encounter the full wrath of Islam. In the event, little was done to support the Shah and the subsequent Khomeini regime denounced both superpowers, the Soviet Union a little less vociferously than the United States. Thus, it can be concluded that however his regime came into being, the effect was to place a blockage upon any substantial Soviet movement. In this context Afghanistan was of course already different in that it already had a Marxist government before the fall of the Shah. Nevertheless, it must be recorded that mujahedin leaders, when interviewed by intrepid Western journalists, preferred to be photographed kneeling upon their prayer mats. Also, elements of fundamentalism became increasingly evident in a wide arc from Turkey, round to China. For instance, Pakistani generals chose orange juice rather than the more familiar nightcaps of the Raj.

The conspiracy theory may be dismissed as *post hoc* rationalization, but it does provide one explanation for a number of disparate events. A more likely possibility is that as events occurred, the possibilities became apparent and the planning involved was comparatively minimal.

Soviet planning

Despite the fact that it is generally considered by international relations experts that Soviet planners tend to think in longer-term increments than their American counterparts, no obvious thread seems discernible in Soviet planning with regard to the Middle East. Much was made of a shortfall in oil production, reported in 1985, but the event has not been repeated and was probably more a result of internal bureaucratic problems than resource exhaustion. Indeed, although the R/P ratio for the Soviet Union is low, it would be expected that with Western technology new fields could be brought onstream in Siberia. Furthermore, there is the obvious potential of offshore oilfields along the gently shelving Arctic coastline. It must also be remembered that, following the events of late 1989, a complete revision of COMECON has occurred. The Soviet Union is no longer treaty-bound to supply oil to satellite states at subsidized rates. As a result, it has the choice of conserving its resources or obtaining hard currency for them. Thus, it can be concluded that any reasons the Soviet Union may have had for casting rapacious glances towards the oilfields of the Middle East are now less compelling.

It must be remembered that during the long period of the cold war the two superpowers were at great pains to avoid direct confrontation. Conflict may have occurred between surrogates, but a Soviet–American 'eyeball-to-eyeball' was meticulously avoided. Therefore, unless oil shortfalls were desperate, it seems very unlikely that the Soviet Union ever intended risking conflict over Middle Eastern oil. Indeed, the Carter declaration left very little doubt as to what the United States' reaction might have been to a Soviet advance into the oil-rich Gulf countries. With hindsight, it can be seen that Soviet policy tended to be pragmatic and, in particular, to capitalize on natural instability.

United States' threat

While it is reasonable to conclude that at the superpower level Western perceptions have focused upon a Soviet threat, the feelings within the Gulf have been different. Arab perceptions, based upon the oil question and relationships with Israel, have been that the United States poses a far greater threat. The Carter doctrine appeared somewhat ambiguous in that it seemed to offer protection to US and allied oil supplies rather more than to Arab oil producers. Internal political changes affecting oil supplies would be treated in much the same way as external threats. Furthermore, compared with the Soviet Union, the apparent lack of planning displayed by the United

States in its conduct of foreign affairs constitutes a source of worry.

However, the major factor underlying all geopolitical concerns in the Arab world is that of Israel. Feelings about the United States tend therefore to be ambivalent. While sustaining Israel through its military, political, economic and psychological support, the United States remains the one power in the world which can force Israel to negotiate. If the Israeli–Arab confrontation is ever to be settled peacefully, it can only be through the good offices of the United States.

Initially, the new Bush administration seemed to be set on pressing for Israeli–Palestinian negotiations, but its resolve faltered in the face of fierce opposition from the newly elected Likud government of Shamir. One result has been a general feeling of hopelessness among Palestinians, given expression in support for Saddam Hussein and the increasingly military nature of the Intifada. While the actions of Iraq have produced one cleavage in the Arab world, US actions have undoubtedly produced another. Central Command exercises, together with US aid, have split off Egypt and Oman, the only countries to supply bases. The immediate thrust of US diplomacy has resulted in the huge build-up of US forces in Saudi Arabia. This may have brought some stability to the local area, but the net result must be destabilizing to the Arab world as a whole. Indeed, it seems a reasonable assumption that should serious fighting begin, the cleavage produced by the Iraqi action will close much more rapidly than those produced by US foreign policy.

The United States and the West in general is left with a continuing moral dilemma. To intervene against the wishes of a legitimate government offends against one of the basic tenets of Western civilization. Presumably, in the cases of Panama and Grenada, this tenet was overlooked or, possibly, the governments were considered illegitimate. The West has always tended to characterize such behaviour as morally wrong. Unfortunately, potential for such action will continue to emerge in this era of resource geopolitics. In a much-publicized article, Francis Fukuyama wrote of 'the end of history'.[3] In his spirited defence, he clarified the position by asserting that no other 'great idea' is likely to challenge liberal democracy. However, he particularly noted that nationalism and fundamentalism were powerful and growing forces which were likely to produce conflict situations. Thus, rather than major confrontations, local crises are the more likely outcome during this period of history.

Regional conflicts

There are many actual and potential conflicts in the adjacent areas of the Middle East which could spill over and threaten regional conflict within the Gulf and Arabian Peninsula. The longest-running and most serious is of course the Israeli–Arab confrontation, which has dominated the geopolitics of the Middle East since at least 1948. Apart from the continuing saga of minor incidents, cold war has turned to hot war on three occasions: 1948, 1967 and 1973. Additionally, there was military action against neighbouring Arab states in 1956 and 1982. The significance of the issue is that it interests all Arabs directly and provides them with their most obvious focal point. The Arab states are, in general, so disparate and differ so widely in viewpoint that unanimity on any subject is difficult to achieve. However, such a state has been achieved with regard to Israel and Arab states continue to behave as if Israel did not exist. Therefore, since all are so psychologically and spiritually involved, any action by Israel is likely to produce a response throughout the Arab world. This, of course, is the explanation for the generally subdued performance by Israel during the Iraq–Kuwait crisis.

Nevertheless, it must be stated that among the Arabs there is a certain ambivalence towards the Palestinians. Palestine remains one of the few entities to be completely removed from the world map since the Second World War. This is all the more remarkable since during this period the general trend has been in the opposite direction with the proliferation of new states. Despite its formal lack of territory, the Palestine Liberation Organization is accepted as a representative government by the United Nations. The Intifada has of course kept world media attention focused upon the Occupied Territories, but little assistance has been forthcoming from other Arab states. Indeed, Palestinian refugees, after those from Afghanistan, the largest such body in the world, tend to inspire less than fraternal feelings. In many cases, this amounts to actual hostility. Such reactions probably result from the levels of education and sophistication of the Palestinians, which are often in sharp contrast to those of the local people. In this way, their history shows remarkable parallels with that of the Jews. As a result of the three wars, there has been a Palestinian diaspora and, as a non-territorial people, security and advancement could only be achieved through learning. The main legacy of the continuing Israeli–Arab strife, the refugees, are generally considered to constitute a threat to stability in the Gulf.

The war in Lebanon has been geographically limited in scale. The regional impact has resulted from the identification of other states with the warring factions, variously described as anything from terrorist groups to freedom fighters. In particular, the support of Iran for Hezbollah and Syria for Amal has produced tensions. The capturing of Western hostages has maintained media attention on the conflict. However, the situation and the changing relationships alter constantly and any spill-over to the region seems unlikely.

The war in Ethiopia to prevent the separation of Eritrea is similarly confined geographically. Notwithstanding, the Ethiopian government remains Marxist and is supported, if only spiritually, by the Soviet Union. The Eritreans are Arabs and have received help from several Arab countries, including Sudan. It has been reported that relations between Israel and Ethiopia have been strengthened as Israel fears an Arab Red Sea hegemony. On the other hand, any practical assistance with regard to irrigation projects on the Nile would put at risk the Camp David Accords, as Egypt is particularly sensitive to any hydraulic developments within the Basin.

The Kurds are divided between five countries: Turkey, Iraq, Iran, Syria and the Soviet Union. Through their desire to achieve nationhood, they have been continually involved in conflict. Such apparently small-scale hostilities are unlikely to exercise any major influence on the region as a whole, but they could be unwittingly involved in larger-scale warfare as a result as their role as pawns. During the Iran–Iraq war, both belligerent governments played their Kurdish card. In the event of water problems in the Tigris–Euphrates Basin, Iraq could well repeat the process against Turkey.

Current unrest amongst the Muslims of the south-central states of the Soviet Union may spread further afield, but seems unlikely to have major Middle East repercussions. Geopolitically, their position can be contrasted with that of Eastern Europe. Whereas the developed countries of Western Europe can provide support, the neighbouring countries to the south-central states are Iran and Afghanistan, both attempting to recover from prolonged warfare. Thus, the Muslims of the Soviet Union will, for the time being, need to retain ties with the central government.

Within the Arabian Peninsula itself, there is always some potential for friction between Saudi Arabia and its much smaller neighbours. However, the foundation of the Gulf Cooperation Council (GCC) in 1981 provided a forum and a framework for joint cooperation. The only situation in the Peninsula which could be described as potentially hostile is that between the only peripheral state not in the GCC, Yemen, and Saudi Arabia. While the Yemenis have genuine claims on contiguous areas of Saudi Arabia, particularly Asir Province, any regional spill-over conflict is likely to result more from Yemeni support for Iraq during the Iraq–Kuwait crisis.

The two long-running wars in the region, that between Iran and Iraq and that in Afghanistan, both ended in the late 1980s, the former in 1988 and the latter in 1989. Since in each case there was an element of superpower rivalry, both might have resulted in a wider conflagration. However, legacies remain. Impoverishment resulting from the war, unemployment and a declining oil price were all contributory factors, leading to the take-over of Kuwait by Iraq. In the case of Afghanistan, although many of the four million refugees have managed to return home, there are still large tented villages in Pakistan and, to a lesser extent, Iran. As the world spotlight has moved from the area, less aid is forthcoming and friction between the refugees and the native population is likely to grow.

Arab nationalism

The development of Arab nationalism has already been described in detail. The limitations of the concept of Pan-Arabism are all too obvious. There are such vast discrepancies between the Arab countries, ranging from such factors as size, population and wealth to religious adherence and social custom. There is basically a common language, but even this is not easily comprehensible from one end of the Middle East to the other. Thus, the integration of the Arab world poses almost insuperable problems and those who have attempted it, such as Nasser and Gadaffi, have never succeeded in uniting more than two countries at any one time. Nonetheless, Pan-

Arabism constitutes an emotive appeal, likely to be used by regional demagogues such as Saddam Hussein.

Indeed, the Iran–Iraq war was characterized by the Iraqis as a conflict between the Arab and the Persian world. The result of such emotional language, but more importantly, the immediate threat of the Ayatollah Khomeini, persuaded the wealthier Gulf states to support Iraq in the conflict. Arab nationalism is seen more obviously in the major struggle against Israel.

Not only do the Arab countries differ considerably from each other, but they are geographically comparatively far-flung. The obvious focal country through which Arab unity might be generated is Egypt. However, the Camp David Accords were strongly opposed by fellow Arabs, with the result that the country was marginalized. It was only in the late 1980s that, under Hosni Mubarak, Egypt was able to regain lost ground. Saudi Arabia is the guardian of the holy places, but with its rigid internal structure, enormous wealth and very small population is atypical and unsuited for leadership. Syria lacks the population and prestige of Egypt and is not oil-rich. This leaves, of the centrally placed larger countries, only Iraq, which moved to establish its credentials by the annexation of Kuwait. However, among the many results of this was the alienation of a large part of the Arab world. How long this will continue depends very much upon the long-term outcome of the Iraq–Kuwait crisis.

Ideologies

With the demise of Marxism–Leninism world-wide, the major ideological confrontation of the twentieth century has all but disappeared. Although China remains very much in the socialist camp, the future orientation of the Soviet Union is in doubt and further export of Marxism–Leninism or its derivatives to the region looks very doubtful. Nonetheless, certain ideological divisions remain.

The most obvious division, that between the Yemen–Arab Republic and the People's Democratic Republic of Yemen, evaporated on 22 May 1990 when the two countries executed a low-profile merger. Ideologically, it appears, the new Yemen is a direct continuation of the Yemen–Arab Republic. This has simplified to a degree the complex ideological situation which formerly dominated the riparian states at Bab el Mandeb. The position on the southern shore is less clear. Ethiopia, still a Marxist state, may change its political alignment gradually, as was the case with Afghanistan, or suddenly, as happened in the People's Democratic Republic of Yemen. It may also fragment if Eritrea is successful in establishing itself as a separate entity. At the moment, Djibouti and Somalia remain, if not quiescent, Western-orientated.

Marxism–Leninism may have largely disappeared from the region, but totalitarianism remains. The Gulf Cooperation Council countries all remain autarchies, each ruled by a tiny hereditary élite. They can be classified as totalitarian in that the rulers are absolute monarchs and govern by decree. They may have an advisory council of ministers, but in most cases, these are members of the immediate or extended family. Alone among them, Kuwait practised limited democracy with an extremely restricted franchise of some 60,000. Israel is a limited or guided democracy, with some restrictions on voting rights. Turkey, which has alternated between military rule and elected government, has the only truly democratically elected leadership in the region.

An interesting development has been the re-emergence of the theocracy. The foundation of Israel is closely connected with Judaism, but the nature of the state is essentially secular. In contrast, the Iranian revolution under Ayatollah Khomeini, produced a genuine theocracy. To an extent, this has been subsequently modified, but the pivotal role of Islam is unchallenged. Furthermore, the fundamentalist approach clearly has an appeal, particularly to the poorer members of neighbouring societies. In Turkey, for instance, a state deliberately secularized by Ataturk, fundamentalism is perceived as a definite threat. The export of fundamentalism from Iran may occur, therefore, not through force of arms but through more subtle means. The newly elected fundamentalist government of Algeria may well be the first example of this diffusion process.

The fifteen to twenty rulers in the Gulf states who control such a high proportion of the world's oil resources pose an interesting problem for the long-term stability of the region. At the moment, they hold complete power, are recognized as legitimate and are fully supported by the West. Given the pressures for democratization, they may either resist or gradually change their role. In the Far East, for example, this has been effected by the development of corporations, so that princes have been transformed into executives. One long-term effect of the Iraq–Kuwait crisis is likely to be greater pressures for the development of democracy. Many of the expatriate workers come from democratic countries such as India and therefore there is some acquaintance with the idea of democracy.

International boundaries

The Middle East poses particular problems with regard to the drawing of land boundary lines. The key resources on which life and wealth depend are water and oil, both obtained from underground sources. Thus, the position of a line at the surface can be critical for oil or water abstraction. The disputed Iraq–Kuwait boundary is a case in point, since its exact location influences the exploitation of the Rumeila oilfield, one of the twelve mega-oilfields outside the Soviet Union. The boundary between Oman and the United Arab Emirates, which separates Buraimi and Al Ayn, provides a good example of a water problem. Excessive water use in Al Ayn has, over the past decade, been lowering the water table at some five metres per year under Buraimi. In most cases in the region, international boundaries were not constructed to reflect the distribution of subterranean resources. Thus, they are merely likely to exacerbate resource geopolitics.

A second problem concerns, for the most part, the lack of easily identifiable permanent surface features. Boundary demarcation across a relatively featureless landscape obviously poses difficulties. Even if the actual line is settled, its exact position on the ground may lead to dispute.

There are a number of stages in the definition of boundaries and there are examples in the Middle East of each stage. The allocation of a boundary entails the broad agreement as to the zone through which it will pass. With further negotiation, the specific position may be drawn on a map, during the stage known as delimitation. Finally, if the position is monumented on the ground, the stage of demarcation has been reached.

In the Arabian Peninsula, the complete boundary between Oman and Saudi Arabia and most of that between Yemen and Saudi Arabia has not been allocated. That between the United Arab Emirates and Saudi Arabia has been allocated and delimited, but not demarcated. The boundaries separating Saudi Arabia from Kuwait, Iraq and Jordan have all been allocated, delimited and demarcated. The boundary between Kuwait and Iraq is, at least in its northern sector, disputed. Other boundaries, currently or recently the subject of dispute, are those between Iraq and Iran at the Shatt al Arab and between Libya and Chad in the area of Western Sahara. The eastern section of the boundary of Israel and the internal boundary of Cyprus are both classified as armistice lines.

Given the significance of oil and water and the general lack of boundary definition, it can be readily appreciated that disputes over land boundaries pose a continuing threat to peace in the Middle East. Furthermore, there remain nomadic tribes throughout the region and their movements illustrate the problems of border control. The Libya–Chad boundary dispute was referred to the International Court of Justice in September 1990 and it seems likely that a similar dispute between Yemen and Saudi Arabia will be referred in the near future. In the case of Iraq and Kuwait, the dispute involves oilfield exploitation, the vulnerability of the approaches to a port and a defensible coastline. It seems likely that some compromise, which will partially alleviate the problems of Iraq, will be reached.

Since, with the exception of the Atlantic and Indian Ocean coastlines, there are almost no areas of the Middle East with a 400-nautical-mile width between countries, offshore boundary negotiation is almost always necessary. Sixteen boundaries have already been settled, half of them in the Persian/Arabian Gulf. Most of the median line of the Mediterranean and the Red Sea has yet to be negotiated.

The problems are if anything more complex than those which obtain with land boundaries. The position of any line is likely to be critical with regard to oil, gas and other sea-floor resources, but there is no way in which it can be marked other than on charts. The problems of delimitation are basically twofold. Firstly, there are the geographical aspects such as the definition of a base line, what constitutes an 'opposite' coastline and what is the 'natural' prolongation of the land. This last could be particularly significant in the case of the Iraq–Kuwait dispute which involves both offshore and onshore boundaries. Since the two disputed islands, Warbah and Bubayan, are composed of sediments deposited by the Tigris–Euphrates system, they could be said to constitute the natural prolongation of Iraq.

The other key problem in decision-making concerns equity. This entered the dispute in the case of Libya and Malta. Libya has the longest coastline in the Mediterranean, but Malta is so small that it needs to maximize all available resources. In the event, the geographical case presented by Libya overcame the economic plea of Malta and the first part of the boundary was drawn on the Maltese side of the median line.

As land resources are exhausted, those of the sea floor will become more important and boundary delimitation will be vital. With so many resources offshore in the Middle East, disputes are bound to arise over the boundaries. The focus may well be upon the median line down the Mediterranean and either the Persian/Arabian Gulf or, more probably, the Red Sea, which will effectively divide the North from the South.

Water geopolitics

As indicated during the discussion on oil, many commentators would consider that, following the apparent end of East–West confrontation, we are now entering the era of resource geopolitics. For the Middle East this clearly involves oil, but in the long term and for the inhabitants of the region water is a far more geopolitical liquid. This view was reinforced during the build-up of the Iraq–Kuwait crisis when media interest focused very much upon water rather than oil. Not only were there three special documentary programmes on British television, but there were also numerous articles. That by Dominic Lawson (*Sunday Correspondent*, 30 September 1990) was of particular significance in that he suggested that a deliberate constraint should be put upon the water supplies to Iraq to increase pressure on the regime and to bring about a solution to the problem. Fortunately, this was essentially journalistic licence, because blocking the flow of the Tigris or the Euphrates for any length of time would be hydraulically impossible. Since, in January and February 1990, the flow of the Euphrates had been reduced to a trickle as the lake behind the Ataturk Dam was being filled, it was presumed that the water could be switched off relatively easily.

Given this high media profile and the fact that water has only been seriously considered in such a political context since the mid-1980s, this section is more detailed than those in which the other threats were discussed.

While there is some scope for water geopolitics in humid environments, the potential for the use of the 'resource weapon' is obviously highest in areas of scarcity. As the ultimate determinant of water availability is precipitation, regions with an arid climate are those most at risk. Most vulnerable among these, having in general a very meagre rainfall but also a burgeoning population, is the Middle East. In particular, countries of the Arabian Peninsula in which economic and social life is underpinned by oil revenues are those encountering the greatest problems.

Annual rainfall shows great variation, ranging from well below 100 mm per annum in the Saharan and Arabian Deserts to 200 mm around the desert fringes and up to 400 mm in slightly higher areas. Cultivation of any kind requires at least 400 mm, while areas with less than 250 mm can provide only rough grazing. The major exceptions to this pattern occur in the higher mountain areas and along the Black Sea and Caspian Sea coasts. In many of these areas falls of over 1000 mm, in places 2000 mm, per annum are recorded. Thus, it is basically only where relief intervenes that the Middle East is suitable for agriculture. Furthermore, the lower the annual total, the less reliable the rainfall becomes, so that several years of drought may be followed by the incidence of catastrophic floods. Dewdney, in the *Cambridge Atlas of the Middle East and North Africa*, provides a transect to illustrate this point (Table 5.1).[4] This table illustrates not only the very large range in possible totals throughout the region, but also the increase in variability as the mean total decreases.

Table 5.1 Annual precipitation in the Middle East (mm)

Station	Mean total	Maximum total	Minimum total
Rize	2440	4045	1758
Konya	316	501	144
Baghdad	151	336	72
Cairo	22	64	1.5

Rainfall annual variability exercises a profound influence upon the success or failure of agriculture, particularly in the marginal lands. Water scarcity can change to water abundance and rapidly revert to water scarcity. Despite every effort to enhance groundwater, there will in flood periods be inevitably large losses to the sea or to an interior basin. Along the Batinah coast of Oman, this loss is put as high as 80 per cent.

These water problems must be assessed in the light of the comparatively high rates of population increase throughout the Middle East and the resulting need for increased economic development, particularly in agriculture and industry. Thus, the move towards self-sufficiency in food is, in most countries, severely constrained by water problems. The necessity to use all possible sources and to develop new supplies is clearly recognized in the priority given to water policy by all the governments of the region. There is a high level of investment in water exploration, the construction of hydraulic structures and the development of alternative supplies.

The full potential impact of the problem can be appreciated using population projections.[5] Table 5.2 lists figures for water availability, both surface and ground and if the accepted minimum of 1000 m^3 per capita per annum is taken, the shortfall in the Middle East at present, particularly in the year 2000, is clear. To avert the potential crisis, all water sources — surface, ground and artificial — must be investigated and utilized. However, climate past or present exercises the ultimate control of the first two sources. It is only with regard to the third source that man has some freedom, but this at present is largely tempered by economics.

Table 5.2 Water availability in the Middle East (per capita in 1000 cu.m per annum)

	2000	Population increase (%)
Algeria	1.0	111
Arabian Peninsula States	0.3	106
Cyprus	0.05	22
Egypt	0.05	111
Iran	2.5	145
Iraq	1.3	173
Libya	1.2	198
Morocco	0.9	132
Sudan	1.9	107
Syria	1.0	165
Tunisia	0.4	126
Turkey	2.3	118

Water scarcity

Throughout very large areas of the Middle East and virtually all of the Arabian Peninsula there is no permanent surface flow. All of the perennial rivers, with the exception of the Nile system, are to the north of latitude 30°N. Indeed, even beyond that parallel, there are considerable areas with only ephemeral surface flow. Furthermore, the Nile itself receives most of its discharge from rain which falls outside the region on the upland plateaux of East Africa and the highlands of Ethiopia.

The predominance of intermittent flow poses a number of basic problems. The measurement and monitoring of such flow presents practical difficulties. Instruments deployed might only be operational for a few hours in several years and during that time they might need to withstand enormous pressures from water and transported material. It is therefore inefficient to use expensive high-technology equipment, but low-technology devices are still largely in the development stage and indirect methods yield only approximate values. As a result, data on run-off per unit area are still scarce within the Middle East and only for permanent rivers can reliable statistics be given. The estimated total annual mean flow of major rivers (in billion cu.m) ranges from 84 for Egypt, 80 for Turkey and 76 for Iraq, to 28 for Syria, 1 each for Israel and Lebanon and 0.5 for Jordan.

A second result of the comparative lack of surface flow is that the opportunities for barrage construction are limited. The majority of the perennial rivers have one dam and multiple damming is becoming the norm. All dams, but particularly the large multi-purpose variety, can of course exercise a great influence on development downstream, since they affect both the quantity and the quality of the water. The situation may be further exacerbated if the lower reaches of the particular river are in a different state. For example, the largest in the region, the Ataturk Dam on the Turkish section of the Euphrates, will, when it is completed in about 1991, have a capacity to irrigate some 727,000 hectares.[6] Both in operation and particularly during the period of reservoir filling, this scheme must exercise a profound influence upon the various irrigation projects in Syria and Iraq. There are at least thirty-five major dam schemes projected for the permanent rivers of the region, but the increasing tendency is towards construction on ephemeral rivers. In a few cases, these may be designed to impound sufficient water for a permanent reservoir, but at worst they are intended to check loss and enhance recharge. For example, the Saudi Arabian programme included the provision of some sixty such dams of varying sizes by 1990. Already in Oman two major recharge dams have been constructed on the Batinah and, at present, feasibility studies are being conducted on Salalah Plain for further installations.

The accent on recharge illustrates the importance which has, for millennia throughout the region, been attached to groundwater. In the Middle East, two major categories of aquifer have been distinguished, the shallow and the deep. Shallow alluvial aquifers are located sediments below wadis and river valleys, and beneath alluvial fans and plains. Since they are mostly unconfined, their water tables respond rapidly to changing climatic conditions. The deep rock aquifers are usually limestone or sandstone but, as they reach capacity abstraction, increasingly of suitably fractured hard rock. These aquifers are frequently confined and extend over far greater areas than the shallow aquifers. Furthermore, particularly if the area of outcrop is limited, recharge rates may be very slow. As a result, they may contain water which can, in places, be many thousands of years old. Shallow aquifers may be found throughout the region, but the major deep aquifer systems are limited to the Arabian Peninsula and North Africa.

Commonly, water is obtained from springs and wells, in the latter case using lifting devices which vary from the most primitive to modern diesel pumps. In many Middle Eastern countries but particularly Iran and Oman, canals largely subterranean known as qanats or aflaj, have been constructed. The dramatic increases in water requirements over the past two decades have placed a great strain upon all of these sources, and this is reflected in the high levels of investment in water technology. Since aquifers react to change comparatively swiftly, overpumping inevitably results in a fall in the level of the water table which may lead to the complete desiccation of springs, wells and qanats. The situation is rendered even more fraught in that over the greater part of the region the extent of individual aquifers, and especially the rates of recharge, are largely conjectural. If, in addition, wells are sunk to draw on the same aquifer as a spring or a falaj, the competition must lead to rapid resource depletion. This has happened in Oman and it can produce not only economic but also social and political disruption which limits development locally. Whereas a well which is usually owned by one family and from which water can be drawn as required hinders competition, a falaj, owned or controlled by a village or similar settlement, requires essentially cooperative activity for the equitable distribution of the water.

As increasing quantities of water are withdrawn, the groundwater pressure landward is reduced and this may allow the incursion of saline water from the coast. Through this mechanism, the fresh water supply of Bahrain has been virtually totally destroyed and even along the Batinah coast of Oman there are marked increases in salinity. In the case of Egypt, the reduced water levels in the Nile have led to a decline in normal recharge and the encroachment of salt water to some 20 km inland. The deep aquifers, particularly those containing 'fossil water', pose their own problems, one of which concerns whether or not the resource is renewable. Many authorities consider that the abstraction of the older deeper water is effectively a branch of the mining industry. The most spectacular example of this is the Great Man-Made River project in Libya, which is intended to irrigate some 18,000 hectares. If there is no replenishment to the aquifer, the life of this project must be of limited duration.

A further issue concerns the quality of water extracted from deep aquifers. It tends to be frequently brackish and to require desalting. An alternative to the construction of desalination plants at the extraction point is to transport water and mix it with desalinated water produced elsewhere, to provide a suitably potable 'cocktail'.

Surface water sources, scarce as they are in the region as a whole, are approaching capacity utilization, and with groundwater in many areas approaching exhaustion there is great urgency attached to the search for alternative sources. Chief among these by far has been desalination and the present world installed capacity can produce over three billion gallons per day from some 5700 plants. More money has been spent on installations in the Middle East than any other part of the world and indeed 60 per cent of all the plants currently in operation are in the Arabian Peninsula. These are predominantly multi-stage flash (MSF) plants, but other methods, such as reverse osmosis (RO), electro-dialysis (ED) and vapour compression desalination (VCD), are being introduced. Running costs vary from approximately $1.7 to perhaps as low as $0.7 per m^3. Other developments in the Middle East include the introduction of hybrid plants using, for example, membranes and distillation. The first of these was established at Jubail, producing 15 million gallons per day at a cost of $2.75 per gallon per day installed capacity. Another source of 'artificial water' is that produced from the treatment of sewage. So far, use of such water has been limited to irrigation, particularly of amenities. At the present time, most use of recycled water has been made in Jordan, Qatar, Kuwait and Saudi Arabia.

Water restrictions

The restriction of water supplies can result from both the indirect and direct actions of man. As already discussed, over-pumping can result in saline incursions and also the desiccation of springs and qanats. Aquifer contamination can also occur through spillages or deliberate dumping. In many parts of the Middle East, the pace of modern convenience living has far outstripped the capacity for waste disposal. Wadis frequently provide convenient disposal areas and, as a result, toxic substances may enter the water system. With increasingly intensive agriculture, surplus additives such as fertilizers and sprays can seep down to the water table. Serial irrigation down a valley, with the use and reuse of the same water, also leads to an increase in dissolved substances. Through his normal activities, therefore, man is likely to reduce usable water supplies and thereby limit development.

However, by far the most significant acts of man are those which are deliberate and geopolitical. Among these, the most obvious and those presenting the greatest problems, both potential and actual, are those involving the distribution of surface water. Whenever a catchment is divided between states, there is always the possibility of conflict. Since abstraction affects both the quality and quantity of water available to downstream users, unless there are ample supplies throughout the year, some agreement about sharing is required. Political control remains with the upstream state, but whether or not disputes spill over into conflict depends not only upon the relationship between supply and demand, but also upon the relative strengths and particularly the water-need perceptions of the various states.

The number of shared continental basins in Africa is 57, totalling 60 per cent of the area of the continent and in Asia the number is 40, accounting for 65 per cent of the area. For example, the Jordan Basin comprises 11,500 sq. km. The percentage of the area of each riparian state within the basin is: Jordan 54, Syria 29.5, Israel 10.5 and Lebanon 6. Apart from that of the Jordan, the other two major international basins within the Middle East are those of the Nile, shared by four countries, and the Tigris–Euphrates, divided principally between three.

The Nile system drains 10 per cent of Africa and, within its basin, are nine riparian countries. No other river flows through so many different climatic regions and as a result it has the most complex hydrological regime. In particular, there is a major contrast between the seasonal flow of the main stream, the White Nile, and the two major tributaries, the Blue Nile and the Atbara. Thus, contributions to the total flow by the various source countries are extremely difficult to apportion, since there are considerable variations in discharge, not only during the year, but also from year to year. However, it is generally agreed that Ethiopia accounts for between 80 and 90 per cent of the flow and is therefore the key source.

At the opposite end of the basin, Egypt, with a burgeoning population that at present numbers some 56 million, is the key consumer. Water requirements are crucial to every facet of life and it is therefore hardly surprising that estimates for future demand vary widely. For the early 1990s, the Egyptian Master Water Plan foresees a surplus of approximately 8000 million cu.m per year, while the Waterbury assessment indicates a deficit of 4000 m.cu.m annually. In the case of Sudan, a much smaller consumer, but a rapidly developing country, the statistics are even less reliable. Indeed, for the same period, deficits as high as 14,000 m.cu.m per year have been forecast.

At the Egyptian border, the average annual discharge of the Nile is approximately 85,000 m.cu.m and, under the Nile Waters Agreement (1929), Egypt received 48,000 m.cu.m and Sudan a mere 4000 m.cu.m annually. This left approximately one-third of the discharge to pass to the Mediterranean.

This Agreement remained unchallenged for about twenty years until, in the 1950s, tension increased as a result of the controversy over the Aswan High Dam project. Relations deteriorated so far that military confrontation occurred in 1958, but under a new regime in Sudan an Agreement for the Full Utilization of the Nile Waters was signed in 1959. In 1971, the Aswan High Dam was completed, yielding an additional 32,000 m.cu.m of available water from which 10,000mcm was lost annually through evaporation. Of the remaining 22,000 m.cu.m, Egypt received 7500 m.cu.m and Sudan 14,500 m.cu.m annually. Thus, the total yearly water allocation to Egypt is 55,500 m.cu.m. The major scheme to enhance supplies, that of the Jonglei Canal, which would have produced a further 4700 m.cu.m, has been abandoned as a result of civil war in Sudan.

In such a basin as the Nile, where there is already a high level of utilization and demands are increasing sharply, hydropolitics is likely to play a part in future developments. At present, the chief concern focuses upon Ethiopia, the main source of discharge, which is in desperate need of greater food production. This is only likely to be achieved through irrigation, but abstraction in the head waters would clearly reduce the possibilities for development lower down the valley.

The Tigris–Euphrates system is the only one of the three where there is a marked surplus of water. None of the three riparian states, Turkey, Syria and Iraq, is facing an imminent water shortage. The major source of discharge is Turkey, while the major user at present is Iraq. However, both Syria and Turkey are fast-developing economies and both are involved in a number of major water projects.

Although flow fluctuates considerably, the overall discharge of the system approximates to that of the Nile. The mean annual flow of the Euphrates is approximately 32,000 m.cu.m and that of the Tigris 42,000 m.cu.m, although figures produced by the government of Iraq give somewhat higher values. The first major hydraulic construction, the Hindiya Barrage, was built in what is now Iraq in 1913. Today almost 50 per cent of Iraq's agricultural area is under irrigation, following the development of many other major schemes. In Syria, also a fast-growing, predominantly agrarian economy, the main constructions comprise the Ath-Thawrah hydro-electricity and irrigation project. However, it is in Turkey that current hydraulic activity is focused. The first scheme, completed in 1973, was the Keban Dam, but this and the other Turkish projects are dwarfed by the Grand Anatolian Project (GAP), which will on completion provide some 50 per cent of the irrigated area and 50 per cent of the power generation of Turkey. Constructions are taking place on both the Tigris and the Euphrates, but the major element is the Ataturk Dam on the Euphrates. The area to be irrigated, estimated at over 700,000 hectares will require 10,000 m.cu.m of water annually. If this volume is added to that projected for Syrian plans and deductions are made for evaporation from the extensive lake surfaces, the Euphrates discharge entering Iraq would be reduced from approximately 30,000 m.cu.m to 11,000 m.cu.m annually. If this were to occur, it would result in a 20 per cent deficit on Iraq's projected minimum requirements. Furthermore, there would be problems for agriculture. The fluctuations in flow would be removed, but much of Iraq's agriculture is geared to periods of flood and low water.

Hydropolitical activity has already occurred in the basin in 1974 when the filling of the lakes behind the Keban and Ath-Thawrah dams coincided, causing a temporary but significant drop of some 75 per cent in the discharge of the Euphrates. Troops were moved to the frontier, but following the intervention of Saudi Arabia the situation was defused when Syria released additional water in June 1975. On 13 January 1990, the flow of the Euphrates was again greatly reduced as the reservoir behind the Ataturk Dam was filled. The governments of Syria and Iraq had both been warned in advance and flow had been enhanced prior to the cut-off, but alarm over water security was immediately expressed. The shortfall lasted for approximately a month and the action, given the current environment, represented an interesting piece of geopolitical symbolism.

Of the various schemes to overcome potential water problems by far the most interesting is that of the 'Peace Pipeline', announced by Turkey in 1986. It is proposed that surplus potable water should be piped from the catchments of the Seyhan and Ceyhan rivers to Syria, the West Bank, Jordan, Saudi Arabia and the states along the southern littoral of the Gulf. It is envisaged by Turkey that the supply would be an additional source of potable water, but the political problems which might result from such a dependence are likely to outweigh any engineering problems. Before such a scheme could be developed, a far higher level of cooperation is required throughout the basin.

With regard to the Iraq–Kuwait crisis, the action of Turkey in 1990 illustrated the fact that, under suitable conditions, the flow of the Euphrates could be greatly reduced. However, any thought of switching off the river totally as part of the UN sanctions programme is, from the engineering viewpoint, not feasible. The water would need to be stored and the obvious storage area, the Ataturk Dam lake, has already been filled. Furthermore, Turkey's Middle Eastern policy is based upon cooperation throughout the basin and any geopolitically inspired denial of water would irreparably damage relations with Iraq.

However, it is the catchment of the Jordan, by far the smallest of the three basins, which is the most volatile in international relationships. It is the one basin in which politically motivated water diversion has been seriously planned. The boundaries within the basin, of course, separate not only Arab states of different persuasions but, more importantly, the Arab world from Israel.

The political complexity is illustrated in the geography. There are three main head waters of the Jordan: the Hasbani, rising in Syria and Lebanon; the Banyas, with springs in Syria; and the Dan, wholly within Israel. The major tributary, the Yarmuk, provides the boundary successively between Jordan and Syria and Jordan and Israel. The river Jordan itself forms the boundary between Israel and Jordan and, to the south, the West Bank and Jordan. Bearing in mind the importance of position geopolitically, it can be seen that in the Jordan valley Syria and Lebanon are upper to Israel and Israel is upper to Jordan. Along the Yarmuk, Syria is upper to Jordan and Jordan to Israel. The two most crucially interested states, from the point of view of water supply, are Israel and Jordan and, as yet, power resides largely with Israel. With regard to groundwater, the West Bank aquifers are vital. Although estimates vary, it has been stated that before the annexation of 1967 Israel obtained some 60 per cent of water from the West Bank and post-1967 the figure has risen to 80 per cent. Certainly, Israeli drilling programmes and particularly the establishment of Jewish settlements in the West Bank have greatly depleted supplies available to the Arabs.

Geopolitically, the key areas are therefore the West Bank, the Golan Heights and southern Lebanon. From its position in Golan, Israel is able to protect the Jordan head waters and control some half of the course of the Yarmuk. It has also constructed six reservoirs. The occupation of southern Lebanon has resulted in Israeli control of the complete Hasbani tributary and access to the Litani.

The complex water geopolitics of the Jordan Basin has exercised a considerable limiting influence on development. Since 1951, with the draining of the Huleh Marshes, there have been border incidents connected with water. The most serious arose as a result of Israeli plans to divert water from the Jordan above Lake Tiberias and from attempts, following the Arab Summit of 1964, to divert the Hasbani, the Banyas or both, wholly through Arab territory. Since 1967, there have been PLO attacks on pumping stations in the Lower Jordan and Israeli raids upon the East Ghor Canal. The area remains tense and the situation is likely to deteriorate as the water crisis worsens. At present, Israel is using at least 95 per cent of its available water and Jordan has virtually no spare capacity. In such an arid zone, this can be described as a zero-sum situation. Any gains by one side must result in equal losses by the other. Thus, small developments become critical and even climatic fluctuations can be suspect.

After the various abstractions, the total discharge of the river Jordan to the Dead Sea is equivalent to about 2 per cent of the annual flow of the Nile or 7 per cent of the Euphrates in Syria. Thus, the volume of water is small in comparison with the other two great basins of the Middle East, but the limitations on development imposed by the constant hostility, much of it water-related, are far more significant. Potential incidents between Sudan and Egypt and between Syria and Iraq have in both cases been defused before hostilities actually commenced.

Competition for subsurface water is far less obvious. Nonetheless, as the boundaries of both shallow and deep aquifers do not coincide with political frontiers, there is always potential for conflict. At present, the nearest situation to a border incident occurs between Buraimi (Oman) and Al Ayn (United Arab Emirates). Over the past ten years, over-pumping in Al Ayn has led to a fall in the water table of at least 50 m. As available water becomes scarcer throughout the region, so attention will focus upon the boundaries of aquifers.

As water is both vital and scarce and, since it has already been targeted for resource geopolitics, it can, like petroleum and certain minerals, be considered strategic. In the Middle East, with the quickening pace of development, it is becoming increasingly scarce. Research and development may provide some alleviation of the problems, but any general solution which will remove the threat of geopolitical activity is unlikely to be found until well into the future.

Regional infrastructure

Given the array of regional threats, the infrastructure presents a range of obvious vulnerabilities. International terrorism, state-sponsored and otherwise, has tended to concentrate upon air transport, and there is a growing proliferation of international airports in the Gulf region. There are three international airports within 100 km in the United Arab Emirates alone. Each tends to become a developing hub and thus presents a particularly inviting target. Although over the past ten years the Mediterranean Basin, as the cradle of terrorism, has seen the majority of world incidents, a spill-over into the Gulf region is always likely.

Even more obvious, in many ways, are the sea-lanes, since there are three global choke points within the region. A choke point is a place where geographically or, in some cases, economic constraints result in a concentration of shipping. The most clearly defined world choke points are provided by narrow straits on major shipping lanes. The Strait of Hormuz links the Persian/Arabian Gulf with the Gulf of Oman and the Indian Ocean. Since it is the only exit from the Gulf, it is particularly vital to those states such as Iraq, Kuwait, Bahrain and Qatar, whose only coastal outlets are on the Gulf. It is chiefly important world-wide for the transit of oil and natural gas tankers. The Strait is 39 km wide, but traffic is limited to 1-mile-wide lanes, one in and one out, with a 1-mile separation zone between. Thus, all traffic passes through the territorial waters of Oman, overlooked by the Musandam Peninsula. Musandam, a detached part of Oman, has a tiny population and a small naval base on Goat Island. The depth of the Strait varies from 70 to 90 m and therefore could not be blocked by sunken ships. Some seventy to eighty ships a day transit Hormuz.

Bab el Mandeb, located at the southern end of the Red Sea, is shared between the territorial waters of Yemen, Ethiopia and Djibouti. It is therefore in a region which has seen unrest over the past twenty years. The main channel beyond Perim Island is only 16 km wide and, as with Hormuz, there are separation lanes. The Strait varies in depth from 100 to 200 m and thus, like Hormuz, could not be physically blocked. Approximately fifty-five ships per day transit Bab el Mandeb. Despite the increasing use of pipelines, Hormuz and Bab el Mandeb remain particularly important elements of the petroleum industry infrastructure. As yet, neither has been closed, but both have been the scene of harassment through mine-laying. One result was a steep rise in insurance rates, a constraint virtually as effective as that which might be offered by the possibility of physical damage.

The other choke point, one which has been blocked, is the Suez Canal. The overall length of the Canal is 19.3 km and its width varies from 300 to 350 m. It has a depth of only 17 m and therefore, as evident in 1956 and again in 1967, it can be easily blocked. Furthermore, ships passing through are limited to a maximum speed of 14 km per hour and therefore the average time of passage is some twelve hours. The first phase of the Canal Development Project was completed in 1980 and increased the capacity to ships of 150,000 dwt laden. The second phase would have resulted in a deepening of some 4 m so that ships of 250,000 dwt laden could have transited the Canal. However, this stage has been shelved as a result of a recession in the world oil industry and the increasing use of pipelines in the Middle East.

International pipelines for the movement of oil, natural gas and water represent the other major infrastructural vulnerability in the region. The Iraq–Kuwait crisis has provided an appropriate illustration of the ease with which oil exports can be terminated. With maritime exports prohibited by UN sanctions, and enforced by warships, Iraq retained two other outlets for export. The most important was the pipeline through Turkey to Dortyol on the Mediterranean coast, and the other was a pipeline through the southern fields via Kuwait to parallel the trans-Arabian pipeline across Saudi Arabia to Yanbu. Both Turkey and Saudi Arabia agreed to close off the pipelines. In any level of conflict, pipelines, with their attendant structures such as pumping stations, present obvious targets. Further, if they are damaged, the economic results will be felt almost immediately.

However, even more immediate would be the effects of the destruction of the water infrastructure. As yet, there are no significant international pipelines, although that between Iraq and Kuwait has been completed. Should possible pipelines from the Nile or Euphrates be constructed, the consumer countries would always be vulnerable to supply cut-offs. Should the Turkish Peace Pipeline come to fruition, the number of countries potentially at risk would be very large. On the other hand, the mutual vulnerability would be so great that it would tend to militate against unilateral action.

National threats

Labour migration

A factor which is regionally based but poses a threat, essentially at the national level, is that of labour movements. Throughout most of the post-war period there have been movements of workers, unskilled and skilled, from the oil-poor to the oil-rich countries. Among the most important Arab sources have been Egypt, Jordan and Lebanon, together with the Palestinians. As the economies developed, Arab labour was supplemented by that from South and South East Asia, particularly the Philippines, India, Pakistan and Sri Lanka. Whereas the former group had been used to autocratic regimes and the Arab way of life, the latter was often versed in the ways of democracy. Furthermore, it was this second group which experienced most discrimination with regard to remuneration, accommodation and working conditions. Also, it has been the Indians and Pakistanis who have gradually taken over the middle management roles throughout much of the Gulf. Therefore, they are embedded within and crucial to a system of government which is alien to them and which offers only very limited rewards.

The countries of the Arabian Peninsula operate a sponsorship system which requires all expatriate labour of whatever level to have an indigenous sponsor. This can descend into an iniquitous system in which the non-working sponsor receives a greater income than the worker. The effect is to alienate the more skilled workers and to make the local people work-shy. As a result, when economies decline through price changes or resource exhaustion, and foreign workers cannot be afforded in such large numbers, it will be particularly difficult to sustain government structures.

So sensitive is the issue that for many countries data on the ethnic variations are not published and, in many cases, not collected. In the CIA *World Factbook* (1989) a variety of statistics appears (Table 5.3). The fact that

Table 5.3 Foreign labour in the Gulf, 1989 (%)

Bahrain		Kuwait		Iraq		Iran	
Bahrain	63	Kuwait	39	Arab	75–80	Persian	63
Asia	13	Arab	39	Kurd	15–20	Turkic	18
Other Arab	10	South Asia	9			Other Iranian	13
Iran	8	Iran	4			Kurd	3
						Arab	3

Qatar		Oman		Saudi Arabia		UAE	
Arab	40	Arab	100	Arab	90	UAE	19
Asian	36					Arab	23
Iran	10					Asian	50

Source: CIA, *The World Factbook* (1989), US Government Printing Office, Washington DC.

various bases have been used for these figures can be illustrated with statistics for the non-indigenous labour force (figures in percentages):

Bahrain	Kuwait	Iraq	Qatar	Oman	Saudi Arabia	UAE
58	70	30	85	58	60	80

The extremes, Qatar, UAE and Kuwait, illustrate just how dependent the Gulf economies are upon expatriate labour. Many states have gradually adjusted to allow for foreign cultures, but there remain many substantial difficulties. Although the situation has eased, most immigrant workers, particularly those from the remainder of Asia, are not allowed to bring their families with them. They cannot own homes and their salaries are closely controlled by their sponsors. In general, they owe relatively little to their host societies as they cannot become fully integrated. Moreover, the requirement for expatriate labour will continue. As these countries strive to attain greater self-sufficiency in agriculture, industry and commerce, the local supply of skilled and unskilled labour will never suffice. Although higher education has made great strides throughout the region, Arab graduates and postgraduates tend to gravitate directly into government service rather than the various

Modernization

Education, although frequently not well adjusted to the requirements of the economies, has resulted in a marked generation gap. The older generation, having witnessed the almost instantaneous transition from the camel to the Mercedes, has found adjustment extremely difficult. In many of the countries, apart from the wealthy few who pursued higher education abroad, there are at most two generations who could be described as educated. The changes have been colossal, but even more telling has been the speed of change. This is seen in many facets of life. An increasingly Western consumer life style in the urban areas has created immense service problems. Water and sewage systems have been vastly overstrained and garbage disposal, other than dumping, has in most areas hardly been addressed.

The key issue of wealth distribution and the needs of posterity has produced diametrically opposed views which, in the absence of an electoral system, cannot be reconciled. A major concern is, of course, oil. Some favour continuing rapid development and oil production, broadly following the requirements of Western economies, whereas others favour conservation. Conservation would ensure that the oil wealth remains for future generations, but Arab economies, particularly as a result of the investment of petro-dollars, are adversely affected by any downturn in Western economies.

The long-term problems of the urban areas, great as they are, fade when compared with rural problems. More than that of any other sector of society, the life style of the Bedouins has been almost totally changed. For those who remain migratory, the Toyota pick-up has revolutionized life and brought immense pressures to bear on fragile resources. Those who have sought opportunities in the urban society have been converted from skilled pastoralists to unskilled labourers. In the villages, the lure of oil wealth has led to a migration of able-bodied men and to a consequent decline in agriculture. As a result, agriculture is an extremely minor contributor to all the national economies. Thus, it could be concluded that the rural areas are obsolete. Rural people are subsidized as the true roots of the societies so that some small element of stability can be maintained.

It is perhaps true that with a more broadly based education a better balanced political, economic and social system can be attained. The statistics for literacy (as a percentage), which may well be enhanced, are provided in the CIA *World Factbook* (1990):

Bahrain	Iran	Iraq	Kuwait	Oman	Qatar	Saudi Arabia	UAE
40	48	55	71	20	40	52	68

Again, the bases for these figures probably vary. Kuwait and Bahrain have the longest history of education and development, while the UAE has attracted many educated people, particularly from Yemen.

Religious sects

The basic history of the division between Sunni and Shiia and the later development of the two sects have already been discussed in detail. Over the recent past, fundamentalist behaviour has been associated, almost exclusively, with Shiites who are perceived as a threat within the basic Gulf Arab–Sunni matrix. Such perceptions have, of course, arisen largely as a result of the conduct of the theocracy of Ayatollah Khomeini. Shiites are thought to be potential facilitators of the export of the Iranian Revolution. However, the Shiite population of Iraq, for whatever reason, appeared to remain largely unmoved by the blandishments of Khomeini during the Iran–Iraq war. In Saudi Arabia, the Shiites are concentrated largely in al Hasa province, the oil-rich area. As such, they are viewed as a potential fifth column, but such fears are underpinned by very little real evidence. Francis Fukuyama, as already discussed, foresaw fundamentalism as a key movement, extending beyond the 'end of history'. Many Middle Eastern scholars would characterize this viewpoint as simplistic. Nonetheless, statistics on religious sects are sensitive and, as a result, many are incomplete. The breakdown for the region, provided in the CIA *World Factbook* (1989) is shown in Table 5.4: Iran emerges clearly as the centre of

Table 5.4 Religious sects in the Gulf, 1989

	Shiia	Sunni	Other
Bahrain	70	30	
Iran	93	5	
Iraq	60–65	32–37	
Kuwait	30	45	
Oman			75 (Ibadhi)
Qatar			95 (Muslim)
Saudi Arabia			100 (Muslim)
UAE	16	80	

Source: CIA, *The World Factbook* (1989), US Government Printing Office, Washington, DC.

Shiism, but there are high percentages in Bahrain, Iraq and Kuwait. In the case of Bahrain and Iraq, the rulers come from the Sunni sect, giving a potentially explosive situation. In Kuwait, the rulers are Sunni, but at least they belong to the majority sect. Should Shiite fundamentalism continue to advance, a fact possibly evidenced by the recent assumption of power by a fundamentalist government in Algeria, then the factor of religion poses a threat on the national scale.

Internal system

The autocratic nature of governments throughout the region points to at least long-term insecurity. Iran and Iraq are, in many ways, completely different from the states of the Arabian Peninsula. Both have seen changes of government, although neither has enjoyed democracy, and both have comparatively large populations and potentially some balance in their economies. The Peninsula states, with the exception of (South) Yemen, have always been rigidly hierarchical and have depended almost exclusively, during their modern history, on one commodity. While the oil economy flourishes and salaries and pensions are paid, grievances are unlikely to surface in any extreme form. However, in Bahrain and, to a lesser extent, Oman, oil is already a declining asset.

To continue the development of their economies the countries of the Peninsula will continue to require a large influx of labour, skilled and unskilled. Whether they can become, in the absence of oil subsidies, self-sufficient in agriculture and industry must be highly conjectural. Certainly, the import rather than the home production of food is likely to remain the only choice which is viable economically. Perhaps this state of affairs should be accepted and the oil money invested abroad. Whether a balanced and satisfied society can be maintained on interest payments must be open to speculation. Furthermore, there remains the future of the royal families. It seems unlikely that in the fullness of time their power and rigid control can be maintained. Perhaps their position will metamorphose into that of corporate executives.

Whatever happens, the societies of the oil-rich Arabian Peninsula countries are potentially highly unbalanced. Whether or not there is conflict must depend upon the way that such societies evolve.

Notes

1. pp. 19–20, Brookings Institute, Washington, DC, 1988.
2. pp. 127–129, Macmillan, Basingstoke, 1989.
3. 'A Reply to my Critics', *The National Interest*, Vol. 18, pp. 21–28 winter 1989/90.
4. Dewdney, J.C., *The Cambridge Atlas of the Middle East and North Africa*, pp. 20–21, Cambridge University Press, Cambridge, 1987.
5. Barney, G.O., *The Global 2000 Report to the President: The Technical Report. Volume Two*, Council on Environmental Quality and Department of State, Washington, 1980.
6. Mitchell, J.K., *Cambridge Atlas of the Middle East and North Africa*, op. cit., pp. 24–25.

Chapter 6
The Iraq–Kuwait crisis

Introduction

Kuwait is a small country of 6880 square miles (16,600 sq.km) with about 1.8 million people (1989 estimate). It is bounded on the south by the Neutral Zone and Saudi Arabia, and on the north and west by Iraq. The 130-km border between Kuwait and Iraq has never been demarcated. The main Kuwaiti islands, Bubiyan and Warbah face the Iraqi port of Umm al Qasr and Iraq's sea coast. Bubiyan is about 1.6 km from Kuwait and 8 km from Iraq, while Warbah is about 3.2 km from Kuwait and 1 m from Iraq. These islands are critical to the security of Iraqi oil-loading facilities in the Gulf.

Kuwait is strategically exposed to pressure from Iraq, Iran and Saudi Arabia. It is particularly vulnerable to Iraqi pressure because Iraq can deploy its forces against Kuwait with only short warning. Kuwait was regarded as the main Iraqi supply route from the start of the Iran–Iraq war during which Iraq desperately needed Kuwait's support strategically and financially to sustain its effort against Iran.

Historical background of modern Kuwait

Modern Kuwait had its origins in the middle of the seventeenth century. The rise of the Sheikdom of Kuwait under the ruling Al-Sabah family suggests that the town of Kuwait was built in the early eighteenth century (about 1716). It was in 1765 that for the first time the name of Kuwait was shown on a map produced by the Danish traveller Niebuhr. Before that the name 'Grane' had appeared in European documents used for trading in the region.

Kuwait, as a small trade town, was built by Barrak, the Sheikh of the Bani Khalid tribe who ruled Eastern Arabia in the seventeenth century. Since Kuwait began its march towards independence, the early boundaries of Kuwait have been extended to Jahra village where the wells were superior to those of Kuwait town.[1] The geographical position of Kuwait on the important Persian Gulf and desert caravan trade routes allowed the Kuwaiti merchants to carry goods from Kuwait to the neighbouring countries and the

Mediterranean. This resulted in the growth of Kuwait in the eighteenth century.

During the nineteenth century Kuwait's trade with India and Mediterranean ports continued to increase and the choice of Kuwait by the British as their trading station at the head of the Persian Gulf indicates how stable and prosperous it was.

The absence of any strong centralized rule in Eastern Arabia made it possible for the ruling Al-Sabah to become the first independent Emir of Kuwait. Al-Sabah was chosen by the inhabitants of Kuwait in the tribal manner to administer justice and the general affairs of the town. By the end of the nineteenth century most of the Arabian Peninsula was governed by independent rulers who did not acknowledge the authority of the Ottoman sultans. Instead they established treaties of friendship with Great Britain.

In the Anglo–Turkish Convention of the 29 July 1913, the territory of Kuwait was recognized as an autonomous Kaza of the Ottoman Empire, its territorial boundaries were defined and practical autonomy was conceded to the Kuwaiti Emir, Shaish Mubarak. Mubarak established a clearly independent status, free from Ottoman influences. At the outbreak of the war Mubarak formally denied all connection with the Ottoman Empire.

Relations with the British continued to flourish, although Kuwait was not in any direct or indirect manner controlled by the regional powers: Ottoman, Persian or Wahabis of Arabia. Indeed, Kuwait could not have maintained its independence without having the economic ability and military power to defend itself against any potential aggressor.

Kuwait in the post-First World War period

With the beginning of the First World War when Britain was fighting the Ottomans, Kuwait stood by the agreement signed by Mubarak in 1899 and took the side of the British who were fighting the Ottomans. After Mubarak's death in 1915, Kuwait was ruled by Jabir, who was followed by Salim in 1917. Jabir and Salim followed the example set by Mubarak in allying themselves with the British. In the meantime, they continued trade with Syria and Turkey, which indicates that they made no effort to support the British blockade of the Ottomans. Salim, a strict observer of the Muslim faith was sympathetic to the Ottomans. This attitude towards the Ottomans provoked the British to such an extent that they threatened Salim by declaring that they would not respect the 1899 agreement if Kuwait were subjected to foreign attack. However, Salim was determined to defend the entire territory of his sheikhdom against any aggressors. In the meantime, Abd al-Aziz, the ruler of Najd and al-Hasa, was not willing to accept the 1913 demarcation of boundaries between Kuwait and his domains. The tension between him and Salim increased when Kuwait was attacked by Ikhwan who enjoyed the support of Abd al-Aziz. Great Britain intervened in the conflict and arranged the Uqair conference to solve the problem of the borders between Kuwait and Najd.

In order to understand how the British attempted to solve the problems of the borders separating Iraq, Kuwait and Najd, it is important to examine British relations with each of these countries.

The British gained control of Iraq as a mandate after the end of the war in 1918 and installed Faisal, son of King Husain of the Hijaz, as the King of Iraq. The 1899 exclusive agreement between the British and Mubarak gave the British a free hand in managing the foreign affairs of Kuwait. In Najd, Abd al-Aziz al Su'ud had been a recipient of British financial aid since he allied himself with them against the Ottomans. Therefore it was the British who enjoyed a privileged position in these three countries at the time when Sir Percy Cox was working on a matter of utmost importance: the settlement of differences over mutual borders. A final solution to the problem would give each of these countries internationally recognized borders which would make it possible for them to sign agreements concerning oil exploration. It was urgent for the British to sign contracts with Iraq for the oil-rich Mosul area in northern Iraq. Indeed the establishment of well-defined borders was more important to the British than to the people involved.[2]

The Uqair conference (1922)

The 1913 agreement between the British and the Ottomans agreed the borders of Iraq, Kuwait and Najd. According to that agreement, Kuwait's borders in the south extended to Jabal Munifa, about 160 miles south of its present borders with Saudi Arabia. This agreement was made when Kuwait was run by Sheikh Mubarakal-Sabah, the most powerful ruler in the Arabian Peninsula at the time. The situation was changed when Sir Percy Cox called Iraq, Kuwait and Najd together for a conference to be held at Uqair, the seaport of al-Hasa, in 1922. This conference can be considered as a continuation of an earlier meeting which was held in May 1922 at Muhammara (Khoram-Shahr) on Persia's southern border with Iraq. The meeting had been called to discuss the borders between the territories of the Najd and Iraq. The Al-Muhammara accord, which was signed on 5 May 1922, regulated the Iraq–Najdi borders and adopted the 1913 agreement for the borders of Kuwait with the Najd. Though Abd al-Aziz at first accepted the Muhammara accord, after returning to Riyadh he felt that the terms of the accord were not satisfactory. In his view Iraq had gained lands that had never before belonged to it. He also felt that Kuwait's southern borders with al-Hasa needed some modifications. On the basis of these misgivings, he rejected the Muhammara accord. The stage was then set for another meeting. Following the rejection by Abd al-Aziz of the accord, Sir Percy Cox decided to ask Iraq, Kuwait and Najd to attend a conference in al-Uqair. The main business of the conference was to settle the Iraq–Najd frontier line. Iraq was represented by Sabih Beg, Najd by Abd al-Aziz al Su'ud, and Kuwait by Major J.C. More, the British Political Agent in Kuwait and Sir Percy Cox, the Coordinator and the most influential figure at the conference. After five days of discussion without any progress, Sir Percy Cox, who was determined not to go home without a settlement, took the initiative and informed the parties that he would himself decide on the type and general line of the frontier. This ended the impasse, when at the general meeting of the conference, Sir Percy Cox took a red pencil and very carefully drew on the map of Arabia a boundary line from the Persian Gulf to Jabal Anaisan, close to the Trans Jordan frontier.[3] This gave Iraq a large area of the territory claimed by Najd. He also deprived Kuwait of nearly two-thirds of her territory and gave it to Najd and ignored the previous Anglo–Turkish Agreement which had drawn the Kuwait boundaries. South and west of Kuwait proper he drew out two zones which he declared would be neutral and known as the Kuwait Neutral Zone and the Iraq Neutral Zone.[4] Throughout the talks, Major More, who was supposed to be watching the interests of the Sheikh of Kuwait, had said nothing. Sir Percy's decision was a blow to Sheikh al Jabir of Kuwait.

The Iraq–Najd protocol was signed on 2 December 1922. It defined the exact frontiers, established the Iraq Neutral Zone, and permitted the free movement of nomadic tribes across the frontier, and the use by both countries of wells near the frontier. The results of the al-Uqair conference were satisfactory for Iraq and allowed Abd al Aziz Ibn Su'ud of Najd to gain territory at the expense of Kuwait. Kuwait lost two-thirds of its southern territories that extended 160 miles beyond its present borders. In the meantime, Kuwait's borders with Iraq remained as they stood before the agreement.

Shaikh Ahmad al Jaber had no choice but to sign, very reluctantly, the unfair and unjust agreement. He was informed in April 1923 that the British government had recognized the Iraq–Kuwait frontiers as claimed by him, including the islands of Warbah, Bubiyan, Maskan, Failaka, Auha, Kubbar, Qaru, Naqta and Umm al Maradim, and other adjacent islets. This was identical with the frontier indicated by the Green Line of the Anglo–Turkish Agreement of 29 July 1913.

Kuwait and United Nations membership

Iraq has long held an ambition to exert political and military influence over Kuwait, and this was realized immediately after the British withdrawal from Kuwait on 19 June 1961. On that day Great Britain announced that it was terminating the treaty which it had concluded with the ruler of Kuwait, Sheikh Mubarak, in 1899. The Iraqi revolutionary regime of Abdul Karim Qassem reacted to this British action quickly. On 25 June, Iraq laid claim to Kuwait on the grounds that the sheikhdom was an 'integral part' of Iraq. The Iraqi move brought an immediate response. Kuwait mobilized its small army to the northern boundary and requested Great Britain and Saudi Arabia for help. Kuwait also asked the United Nations Security Council to meet urgently to deal with its complaint that Iraq was jeopardizing its independence. Both Great Britain and Saudi Arabia responded to the request at once by sending troops to Kuwait.

While the Iraqi government tried to convince Arab and world public opinion that Kuwait was an integral part of Iraq, Kuwait rejected the Iraqi claim vigorously by providing evidence that it had never belonged to Iraq. Beginning on 24 July 1959, Kuwait has successively been admitted to the following international organizations:[5] the International Telecommunication Union (ITU), the Universal Postal Union (UPU), The International Civil Aviation Organization (ICAO), United National Education, Scientific and Cultural Organization (UNESCO), and the International Labour Organization (ILO). Membership of these organizations can be interpreted as an international recognition of the independence of Kuwait. On 20 July 1961, the Arab League accepted Kuwait as a member. An important factor related to the recognition of Kuwait as an independent country is the seating of Kuwait in the United Nations. The Security Council closed its sessions on Kuwait without coming to any determination on the question before it: the juridical position of Kuwait as an independent Kingdom or as a part of Iraq. The Arab League took a decision on 20 July 1961 to support the admission of Kuwait to the United Nations and Kuwait was admitted to membership. The state of Kuwait achieved full independence on 19 June 1961. It was able to win the confidence of, and to be recognized by, practically all the members of the United Nations.

In 1963, Iraq recognized the independence and complete sovereignty of Kuwait and specifically accepted the border as agreed in 1932. This agreement came into force on 4 October 1963. It is binding and can be changed only with consent of the legitimate Kuwaiti authorities.

The facts behind the Iraqi invasion of Kuwait

During the early 1970s Kuwait was caught up in the Iraq– Iran dispute over the Shatt al Arab. Iraq's need to find some way to load large tankers without being vulnerable to Iranian military action, and its reliance on a waterway that was subject to silting and placed its ports within Iranian artillery range, led Iraq to seek a less vulnerable location. Iraq could not achieve such security within its own territory or territorial waters. Iraq's coastline was only 38 miles wide, and the only port that was not dominated from the Iranian shore was dominated by the Kuwaiti islands of Warbah and Bubiyan.[6] Having built up its port and naval facilities at Umm al Qasr, Iraq demanded access to Kuwaiti waters and territory to build an offshore oil-loading facility with pipelines crossing Bubiyan. Kuwait refused this demand because of its fear that Iraq may permanently seize the islands. Iraq sent troops into northern Kuwait on 20 March 1973, and occupied the island of Bubiyan, as well as the area surrounding the Kuwaiti border post at Samita, and caused the closing of the Kuwaiti–Iraqi border. However, relations steadily improved after 1975, and Iraq formally abandoned its claim to all of Kuwait.

However, eight years of war with Iran proved the vulnerability of Iraq's only waterway, the Shatt al Arab, and its port Umm al Qasr, so after the ceasefire Iraq planned to have access to a safer port to ensure its oil exports. The only possible answer to the problem was the Kuwaiti islands, Warbah and Bubiyan. In addition, Iraq owed Kuwait a large sum of money borrowed during the war period.

The Iraqi regime opened its claim (late July, 1990) with a conspiracy theory accusing Kuwait and the United Arab Emirates of launching 'an economic war' against Iraq. The case was discussed and almost resolved when the oil ministers met just before the invasion took place. Iraq lost some grounds for war when Kuwait met many of its demands. However, the Iraqi intention of occupying the islands remained. Despite the United Nations Charter which emphasized that all disputes must be resolved exclusively by peaceful means, Iraq invaded Kuwait on the basis of a response to the so-called Kuwaiti uprising of 2 August 1990. The quisling provisional regime lasted just long enough to demand Kuwait's incorporation into Iraq. This scenario was swiftly rejected by the United Nations Security Council which declared the annexation of Kuwait null and void by a unanimous vote.

To justify its aggression, the Iraqi regime started campaigning by producing documentary evidence that the Kuwaiti rulers had accepted Ottoman supremacy in the eighteenth and nineteenth centuries. In particular, Iraq claimed that Kuwait had become part of the Ottoman province of Basra — an assertion that Kuwait contested but which some experts support.

However, it has been documented[7] that any link with the Ottomans was broken off when Kuwait became a British Protectorate in 1899. Turkey, the successor to the Ottoman Empire, agreed to this arrangement in the 1923 Treaty of Lausanne and any claims based on the connection between Basra and Kuwait were dismissed. Before Iraq gained its full sovereignty in 1932, Baghdad formally reaffirmed acceptance of the present boundaries with Kuwait which had been fixed under British guidance. This has been recognized in the Iraqi memorandum.[8]

The crisis

Like some vast, slow moving, potentially deadly game of chess, the Iraq–Kuwait crisis gradually unfolded after 2 August 1990. The contest has highlighted the very different approaches of the Western, chiefly American, and the Arab mind. As Professor Howard Bowen-Jones, former Director of the Centre for Middle Eastern and Islamic Studies at Durham University, observed: 'The Arab never tries to solve a problem, but tries to live with it.' The ensuing play produced a number of moves and counter-moves, but more dominant were the threats and counter-threats. As with chess, at the highest level, the opening is generally slow and the significance of the initial moves is largely symbolic. Any analysis of the crisis and any forecast of what was to come depended crucially upon the signals sent and their interpretation. It is the perception of an event, rather than the reality, which counts. The drama was at first largely cerebral and focused upon a wide range of facets: ethical, moral, economic, political, military and even religious. At any one time, the state of play and the possibilities could be divined not so much from what was happening in the arid landscape at the head of the Gulf, but from the conflict being waged through the media for public support. With such a vast array of variables, the interpretations, even of experts, differed widely and the view of the individual was likely to be coloured by the orientation of the newspaper or television programme, but more importantly by his own life experiences.

Chronology

From 2 August 1990, news of developments in the crisis rarely left the headlines. However, a number of key dates can be identified:

3 August — the Gulf Cooperation Council and Egypt demand troop withdrawal;

4 August — Saudi Arabia apparently threatened; troops put on alert; USA warns against invasion;

5 August — European Community's total ban on imports from Iraq and Kuwait;

6 August — UN announces mandatory sanctions against Iraq, including a global ban on its oil exports;

7 August — the twin pipeline to Dortyol switched off by Turkey, blocking the movement of half Iraq's oil production;

8 August — King Fahd of Saudi Arabia requests US intervention; Iraq announces the annexation of Kuwait;

9 August — Iraq closes its borders, trapping some three million expatriates, predominantly Egyptians and Asians.

10 August — at the Cairo Summit, twelve out of twenty Arab League members vote to endorse UN sanctions and send forces to the Gulf;

12 August — the Palestinian problem is linked to the crisis as Saddam Hussein demands Israeli withdrawal from the Occupied Territories;

15 August — Iraq settles differences with Iran and agrees to the thalweg boundary on the Shatt al Arab;

25 August — the Security Council authorizes the support of sanctions by naval force;

28 August — Kuwait is formally made the nineteenth province of Iraq by Saddam Hussein;

25 September — the Security Council authorizes an air embargo in Iraq;

12 October — the Security Council condemns Israeli violence, following the slaughter of twenty-one Palestinians on the Temple Mount on 8 October;

29 October — the Security Council passes a resolution, stating that Iraq is responsible for damage caused in Kuwait;

18 November — Saddam Hussein announces the release of hostages in batches;

29 November — the Security Council, by a vote of twelve to two, with China abstaining, authorizes the use of force if Iraq fails to withdraw from Kuwait by 15 January 1991;

30 November — President Bush offers Iraq high-level talks on the crisis;

6 December — Saddam Hussein announces the release of all hostages;

24 December — Baghdad threatens to attack British and American interests throughout the world if force is used to drive its troops out of Kuwait;

26 December — Israel pledges to hit back hard if it should be attacked by Iraq;

29 December — Call-up papers were sent to British citizens in the biggest compulsory mobilization of the reserve forces since the Suez crisis;

3 January 1991 — A special French envoy flies to Baghdad and President Bush says that he is ready for 'one last attempt to go the extra mile for peace';

5 January — Iraq agrees to a United States meeting;

9 January — James Baker, the United States Secretary of State, and Tariq Aziz, the Iraqi Foreign Minister, meet in Geneva;

12 January — Javier Perez de Cuellar, United Nations Secretary–General, meets Saddam Hussein in Baghdad;

15 January — UN deadline set;

16 January — The French peace plan falters as the UN deadline expires;

17/18 January — The air war begins;

21 January — Four Iraqi nuclear research plants bombed;

22 January — The Western powers decide to hold Saddam Hussein responsible for war crimes;

23 January — A block of flats in Tel Aviv is hit by a Scud missile;

26 January — United States accuses Iraq of creating 'a vast oil slick in the Gulf';

29 January — Iraq's best military planes fly to Iran;

31 January — Iraqi troops capture Kafji;

1 February — Kafji liberated by Saudi troops;

11 February — Soviet peace move begins;

14 February — American bombers destroy an air-raid shelter packed with civilians, in Baghdad;

16 February — President Bush calls on Iraqis to oust Saddam Hussein;

16 February — Iraq agrees unconditionally, to move from Kuwait, under the following conditions:

(1) a full cease-fire;
(2) the abrogation of all other UN resolutions concerning Iraq;
(3) Israeli withdrawal from the Occupied Territories, including the Golan
     and southern Lebanon;
(4) the Security Council guarantees all Iraq's historical rights on land and
     sea, in their entirety;
(5) withdrawal of all Allied troops from the Gulf within one month of the
     cease-fire;
(6) the overthrow of Kuwait's rulers, the Al-Sabah family;
(7) the Allies to pay the entire cost of re-building Iraq; and
(8) the cancellation of Iraq's $30 billion debts.

18 February — Britain bombs the town of Fallujah, a non–military target;

20 February — President Bush rejects the Soviet peace plan, the main points
of which are:

(1) stage one: complete unconditional Iraqi withdrawal, safety from attack
     being guaranteed by Moscow;
(2) stage two: annexation of Kuwait annulled;
(3) issues such as prisoners of war to be discussed after withdrawal;
(4) all parties guarantee Iraq's territorial integrity; and
(5) international community to deal with the Arab–Israeli conflict.

23 February — Deadline for Iraqi withdrawal from Kuwait, set by President
Bush;

23/24 February — The land war begins;

2 March — Cease-fire declared.

As with so many disputes in international relations, historical evidence can
be quoted to support opposing arguments. The version of the historical
background outlined earlier propounded by the government of Iraq must
also therefore be considered.

Before the First World War, the territory now known as Iraq was part of the
Ottoman Empire, one province of which was that of Basrah. Kuwait, a trading
post with a small area of date gardens, established on the desert shore, was
attached to Basrah Province. British influence in Kuwait began at the end of
the nineteenth century when, to help secure Great Britain's position in the
Gulf, a secret convention was concluded with Sheikh Mubarak of Kuwait in
December 1899. However, the Sheikh later reaffirmed his loyalty to the
Sultan and the Ottoman Empire. By 1913, the Ottoman government was
suffering financial crisis and entered into an agreement with the British
government about Kuwait. The Sheikh was to have enjoyed a degree of
autonomy under the Ottomans and a border line was decided. The onset of
the First World War meant that this agreement was never ratified. During
the war, the Sheikh was actively encouraged to collaborate with the British
cause. As a result, in 1923, the British government recognized the border

between Kuwait and the newly designated state of Iraq. By this time, however, the geographical and strategic significance of Warbah and Bubiyan islands, together with the adjacent coastline, was recognized by the Iraqi government. Subsequently, during the 1930s, there were several exchanges of communication between the Iraqi and British governments concerning whether Kuwait should be incorporated as a virtually autonomous region within Iraq, or whether the islands and coastal strip alone should be either incorporated or rented. Great Britain, however, decided to keep the border line as specified in the earlier correspondence.

The British–Kuwaiti Agreement was declared in 1961 and Kuwait became independent in 1962. Iraq continued to maintain its claims to the whole of Kuwait, but particularly the coastal areas, to provide security for the developing port of Umm al Qasr. A ninety-nine year lease of Warbah Island was considered by the Kuwaitis, and in 1966 the two countries set up a Joint Borders Committee. No agreement was reached, despite several exchanges and in 1973 Iraq proposed that Bubiyan Island be divided into two parts, the east to belong to Iraq and west to Kuwait. Discussions continued sporadically until the early 1980s, but the problem remained unresolved, so that at the Arab Summit, held in Algeria in 1988, Saddam Hussein's expressed wish to conclude the dispute can be seen as the end of a long saga and the beginning of the present crisis.

Since throughout the protracted negotiations (according to the government of Iraq) no agreements on the border were ratified, it can be seen that Iraq has never agreed with the present position of Kuwait. On the other hand, on several occasions it does appear that Iraq would have been satisfied with a strip of the coastline and some share of the two islands. The claim to the whole of Kuwait has therefore largely lapsed. In the light of this, the position taken during the crisis may be interpreted as a bargaining stance prior to withdrawal to a line to the north which would leave the required length of coast and possibly the islands, in Iraqi hands. The more immediate background to the crisis extends from the end of the long and bloody war with Iran, in which Saddam Hussein had seen himself as the champion of the Arab cause. Despite massive financial support from Kuwait and other Gulf states, his economy was largely ruined and in urgent need of renovation. Furthermore, he had, with the end of the war economy, potentially high unemployment and an army of at least one million ready to be demobilized. This was clearly an opportune moment to resurrect the boundary dispute with Kuwait, whom he envisaged as representative of the typically ungrateful Arab world.

Apart from the historical claims, two other factors weighed heavily in his thinking. Firstly, Kuwait had, over at least the past year, pumped oil well in excess of its OPEC quota, thereby helping to drive down oil prices. For any chance of economic recovery, Iraq had calculated that a price of $18 per barrel was an absolute minimum requirement. Over-production in Kuwait and elsewhere had resulted in a drop to as low as $12 per barrel. Also, there was the question of the Rumeila oilfield, one of only twelve mega-fields outside the Soviet Union. This highlights the problem, already discussed, of land boundaries and subterranean resources. The boundary itself is disputed, but most maps show that it cuts across the southern tip of the oilfield. As a result, Kuwait is able to extract oil which may lie in Iraqi territory. Some maps show that the boundary line is south of the oilfield, but this may be because the actual geographical extent of the field is not accurately defined. A second factor, and one closely related to the first, is the evidence that, during the Iran–Iraq war, at least part of the boundary was moved northwards by Kuwait. This claim has been made in literature from the Iraqi Embassy in London, but was given greater credence with a supporting statement made on BBC Radio 4 by the former British Prime Minister, Edward Heath (7 November 1990).

These factors must be seen in the light of contemporary events in the region. Since 1948, for the Arab world, the overriding problem has been that of the Israelis and the Palestinians. The new Bush administration appeared to be moving towards a more even-handed US approach to the problem. However, with the demise of the coalition government in Israel and the return of Likud, under Shamir, the United States seemed incapable of pressurizing the Israelis even to talk to the Palestinians. At the same time, the wave of Jewish immigrants from the Soviet Union, forecast to be at least 750,000 in number, was threatening further the demographic balance in Israel. Again, the United States seemed incapable of drawing the Arabs into any real dialogue. Furthermore, as discussed by Edward Said (Observer, 12 August 1990):

> Arab oil seemed perpetually hostage to local oligarchies in cahoots with Western oil companies and governments, as his own society (i.e. Iraq) suffered the after effects of a war he believed he had fought on behalf of all the Arabs.

Thus, by Said's reasoning, Saddam Hussein was, given petty squabbles and compromises elsewhere, propelled into the leadership of the Arab world. It could be argued that US foreign policy had effectively placed him there. As Edward Said concluded:

> But, I submit, has the Western and especially the American failure not to draw out the Arabs in a real dialogue, to take their hopes and fears seriously, to address their grievances with responsibility and engagement, has this not also contributed to much of what is unattractive in the Arab world, deflected and distorted its development into the politics of revenge, resentment and angry hostility?

It is against this background that the events of 2 August 1990 must be examined. Was the invasion an economically motivated seizure of a militarily weak independent state? Or was it more a desperate move to fly in the face of Western interests and bring greater heart to a resurgent Arab nationalism?

Political signals

For many years prior to the invasion, the main signal sent by the West to Saddam Hussein had been one of enthusiastic, uncritical support. When, in

1982, the exigencies of war forced Saddam Hussein to modify his previously strident anti-US rhetoric, he was promptly embraced by Washington. It was reasoned that a defeat for Iraq would allow the Iranians to instigate revolution throughout the oil-rich Gulf states. Diplomatic relations were restored in 1984 and there followed ever-increasing amounts of finance, technology and intelligence. This support escalated despite the obvious shortcomings of the Iraqi regime. When the USS *Stark* was hit by an Exocet missile fired from an Iraqi aircraft and thirty seven sailors died, the apology was accepted. Furthermore, the United States ignored breaches of arms export restrictions and refused to exact any penalties following Iraq's use of poison gas and, later, nerve gas against Iran. Meanwhile, it was realized that Iraq was maintaining its support for a number of terrorist organizations. Indeed, despite the fact that Abul Abas was openly based in Baghdad and had organized the hijacking of the Achille Lauro during which an American died, the name of Iraq was removed from the official list of countries sponsoring international terrorism and never reinstated.

US–Iraq trade grew from virtually nothing before 1982 to $3.6 billion annually by 1989. Many European governments also joined the unseemly rush to the Iraqi market. In 1989, UK exports to Iraq reached a peak of £450 million, following the doubling of credit guarantees during the previous year. One result has been that Iraq has become one of the world's greatest debtor nations, with debts to the West amounting to some $80 billion and total debts, including those to the Gulf states, amounting to $160 billion. This of course added greatly to the pressures on the Iraqi government.

The money was spent not only renovating the economy, but greatly expanding the range of military equipment. It has been admitted by Pentagon officials (*Guardian*, 2 November 1990) that since 1985 the US Commerce Department has approved $750 million in exports of sensitive US technology, much of it diverted to Iraq's nuclear, chemical and missile programmes. The ban on weapons was broken with the sale, in 1985, of forty-five Bell helicopters and it is through US corporations that the Saad sixteen-missile complex near Mosul has been constructed. Even more crucially, forty German corporations supplied equipment for chemical and biological weapons and, even after the Israeli bombing of the Osirak nuclear reactor in 1981, France continued to supply nuclear technology. Apart from these countries, the Soviet Union, Egypt, Chile and Brazil have all sold arms and aided the military build-up of Iraq.

Much of this was highlighted with the disclosure of the supergun and the seizure of nuclear triggers manufactured in the United States and en route for Iraq. These events caused a sudden decline in what had been an untrammelled and continuously improving relationship with the West. Conditions worsened sufficiently as a result of the execution of Farzad Bazoft, a journalist, that Mossad was able to provide convincing supergun evidence. However, both the US and Great Britain still seemed extraordinarily reluctant to question Saddam Hussein's motives and remained virtually unmoved, even when he used nerve gas against his own Kurdish population. Indeed, it was only days before the invasion of Kuwait that the United States formally prohibited arms and technology sales. Thus, it can be seen that far from restraint being put upon him, Saddam Hussein was encouraged in the development of his armoury and the strengthening of his position as the major power in the region.

The Economist (29 September 1990) identified five key signals which indicated that Saddam Hussein was turning his attention to further conflict. During the Arab Cooperation Council meeting in Amman, Saddam devoted part of his speech on 24 February to a vitriolic attack on the United States. He stated that since the United States was now the only superpower, unless the Arab nation took action, the Gulf would 'be governed by the wishes of the United States'. He went on to suggest that all money invested in the West might be reinvested in the Soviet Union and Eastern Europe. For astute observers this was yet another shot in the Iraqi President's campaign to be master of the Gulf.

On 2 April, Saddam announced that Iraq had developed advanced chemical weapons which could be launched by rocket. He added: 'we will make the fire eat up half of Israel, if it tries to do anything against Iraq.' This signal was clear-cut, but was interpreted by apologists as a warning against a repeat of the 1981 Israeli air strike.

On 28 May, at an Arab League meeting in Baghdad convened to denounce the immigration of Soviet Jews to Israel and to support his previous anti-Israeli speech, Saddam renewed his threats against Israel. Since immediately prior to this an Israeli had killed seven Palestinian workers and the United States had blocked a PLO proposal for observers to be sent to the Occupied Territories, this diatribe was deliriously received. The more important signal followed in a private session, when Saddam denounced certain Gulf states for over-pumping and thereby keeping oil prices low. This, he said, amounted to an economic war against Iraq.

The fourth signal was the most clear-cut and was made during the President's Revolution Day speech on 17 July. In it he climaxed a reiteration of all his previous themes with a ferocious attack on Kuwait and the United Arab Emirates, whose policy of keeping oil prices low was described as 'a poisoned dagger' thrust into Iraq's back. Indeed, in a letter sent to the Secretary General of the Arab League on the previous day, Saddam had accused those two states of being part of 'an imperialist–Zionist plot against the Arab nation'.

Later in the same month, on 24 July, two Iraqi armoured divisions were moved to the Kuwait border. One day later, the American Ambassador, April Glaspie, had her widely reported conversation with the President. Having listened to a diatribe of his grievances, she insisted that 'we have no opinion on the Arab-Arab conflicts, like your border disagreement with Kuwait'. When asked to explain his troop movements towards Kuwait, Saddam's reply included:

> assure the Kuwaitis and give them our word that we are not going to do anything until we meet with them. When we meet and when we see that there is hope, then nothing will happen. But if we are unable to find a solution, then it will be natural that Iraq will not accept death, even though wisdom is above everything else.

Thus, despite the signals, the Bush administration failed to issue a warning to Iraq about the consequences of an attack upon Kuwait. The official assumption was that the tanks were meant to intimidate Kuwait and that even if military action occurred, as in 1961 and 1973, Iraq would withdraw in exchange for payment.

In the event, Saddam Hussein half kept his promise to give talks a chance through a meeting in Jeddah on 1 August. The second round, scheduled for Baghdad on the following day, never took place as the invasion had begun. The military deployment was so well organized that it must be concluded that detailed plans had been laid well in advance.

The invasion

As the tanks moved into Kuwait during 2 August, the West, and indeed the rest of the world, were momentarily transfixed. Both the United States and Great Britain had concluded that Saddam's troop movements were merely 'rain dancing' to put pressure on Kuwait in the negotiations. In 1961, such moves had been taken seriously and Britain had flown paratroopers from Bahrain. In 1990, no such option existed as there were no British troops within the region. Had British forces been mobilized into Kuwait, even in token numbers, prior to 2 August, the situation could possibly have been changed. If entering Kuwait had required combat with British troops, it is just possible that Saddam Hussein would have desisted. Such a trip-wire approach is a potent signal in that it indicates clearly what will follow. In the event, Saddam possibly misjudged the Western response and entered Kuwait unimpeded.

The US response was characteristically strident and intended to defer further advance into Saudi Arabia. The distance from the southern border of Kuwait to the main Saudi oilfields is only some 250 kilometres and, with the subdued landscape of the area, this could have been transited comparatively rapidly. However, as is clearly documented in the first book to appear on the crisis (*Saddam Hussein and the Crisis in the Gulf* by Judith Miller and Laurie Mylroie),[8] the US Administration never did seriously consider that Saddam was about to attack Saudi Arabia. Firstly, he had no claim or pretext of a claim and, secondly, he would have realized that by taking over one-quarter of the world's oil reserves, he would have attracted enormous retribution. Great Britain joined with the United States in warning Saddam against any adventurism in Saudi Arabia. Having completely misread the signals over the original invasion, the British, with no obligations whatsoever to Saudi Arabia, were presumably attempting to salvage something from what had been a very costly error of judgement. Following so closely after the complete misapprehension of the situation with regard to the Falkland Islands, this must cast some doubt upon the efficiency of the Foreign and Commonwealth Office.

His actions split the Arab world. His support was strong among the poor and dispossessed, the Palestinians and the Muslim fundamentalists, together with the people and leaders of Jordan, Sudan and Yemen. Doubtless, the ordinary people in many other Arab countries had a sneaking regard for what he had done. As Edward Said wrote (*Observer*, 12 August 1990):

> He is admired today by many Arabs who also deplore his methods, but who say
> that the world we live in is essentially dominated by powers who invade, grab
> land, attempt to change governments with scant regard for the principles and
> moral imperatives they proclaim exclusively against Arabs, non-whites and
> the like.

Among the most passionate supporters were the Palestinians, throughout all
strata of society. They will recall, that when President Bush sent in the US
forces, he spoke of the 'inadmissibility of acquiring territory by force'. This is
exactly the wording of UN Resolution 242 which, of course, concerns
Palestine.

The issue, however, posed an interesting problem for the Palestinians.
Should the Americans, in the longer term, lose face and therefore influence,
their control over Israel would be considerably lessened and the chances of
a Palestine solution would therefore diminish. On the other hand, should the
UN use of sanctions and later of force prevail, US supporters such as Egypt
and Saudi Arabia would expect in return for their efforts a rapid and just
settlement of the Palestinian issue.

The effects of the invasion were, of course, most obviously felt in Saudi
Arabia. As David Hirst reported (*Guardian*, 14 November 1990):

> The House of Saud finds itself in the forefront of an inter-Arab struggle so vast
> and vicious that, instead of evading problems, it has turned to tackling them
> head-on. It divides the world into friends and foes, those who are for and those
> who are against, with their attitudes to the Iraqi invasion as the single yardstick.

Given the divisions in the Arab world, Saudi frustration concentrated on the
Yemenis, 1.5 million of whom provide the single largest component in the
foreign work force. Feelings have not been helped by geopoliticians who
have written of the dismemberment of the kingdom into at least three
elements. Should Saddam have succeeded, it was considered, Yemen, as a
reward for its support, would receive its former province of Asir. The
remaining Gulf Cooperation Council countries fell into line to support the
UN–US position. Other Arab countries giving support were Egypt and Syria.
However, it must be assumed that Assad at least has been dealing on more
than one level. He may have sent troops to the UN force, but he is well aware
that should Saddam survive, Syria might have to live with an even more
arrogant Iraq. Egypt is of course a major recipient of US aid and therefore
Mubarak had little choice. Whether the Egyptian masses would have
voluntarily followed the UN line must be somewhat conjectural. Indeed,
there was a strong feeling in Turkey, a country uncomfortably adjacent to the
cockpit of events, that once the missiles were in the air the Arab world might
tend to close ranks in support of Iraq.

Throughout the crisis, despite provocation from Saddam Hussein, Israel
remained largely silent. This undoubtedly accorded with the wishes of
President Bush, as nothing would have split the Arab nations from the UN
cause more rapidly than the entry of Israel into the dispute. The major fear
of the Shamir government would seem to have been that Saddam Hussein

and his regime emerged unscathed. In that case, using the fear of Iraqi nuclear weapons development as an excuse, Israel might well have attacked.

World opinion

In the same way that the invasion split the Arab world, the response of the West divided world opinion. Few Arabs, from the sub-literate to the sophisticated, believed the high moral statements intoned by President Bush. For them the issue remained a classic First World versus Third World conflict. As noted by Jill Tweedie (*Guardian*, 3 November 1990), in quoting the opinion of a Palestinian:

> one thing is clear, the West's back again. They have been coming for five hundred years under different hats. The crusader's helmet, the colonial topee. Their envoys in yamulkas, and their oil-men in hard hats. Now it's the crusader helmet again.

They noted, in particular, the double standards, one applied to Saddam Hussein, the other to the Israelis. Both invaded lands over which they had some historical claims, both continued to violate human rights, and both were defying UN resolutions.

Whereas the Arabs respond to any such crisis with mediation, reconciliation and a saving of face, the Western approach tends to be confrontational. There are considered to be principles and these need to be supported rigidly. However, despite Western support for UN–US actions, even within the West, the parallel so quickly drawn between Saddam Hussein and Hitler was taken as simplistic rhetoric. The idea that Western Europe and even the United States might be at serious risk over the actions of Iraq seemed fanciful.

Furthermore, both sides saw many inconsistencies in the stance taken. If the record of three permanent members of the Security Council alone is investigated, this is understandable. The Soviet Union invaded Czechoslovakia, Hungary and Afghanistan, while the United States invaded Grenada, Panama and, in a different guise, Vietnam. Further, the United States has funded moves aimed at destabilization in many parts of Latin America, including particularly Nicaragua. In fact, the United States itself is still ignoring UN orders over the mined harbours of Nicaragua. China invaded Tibet and the issue made very little public impact. Great Britain, of course, has a similar if slightly more dated record and has consistently supported US actions. Despite all the flag-waving therefore, most thinking people realized that the key dimension was that of oil. Some went further and opined that the statement of the US Ambassador actually encouraged the invasion so that US troops could be returned to the region. The effect on oil prices could have been reasonably accurately forecast and thus the net gains from the whole project of countries such as Great Britain, the Soviet Union, Saudi Arabia and Egypt came as no surprise.

Nearer the region, the balancing act of Turkey, part-European and part-

Middle Eastern, provided a particularly instructive illustration. Key elements in Turkey's economy and foreign policy depend upon the development of the major projects in the Tigris-Euphrates Basin. Therefore, a good relationship with Iraq is essential. So it is ironical that Turkey should have been the linchpin of Western strategy. By closing off Iraq's major oil export route, Turkey, more than any other country, implemented sanctions. Subsequently, it attempted to maintain a low profile in the crisis, despite allowing bombers to fly from NATO bases on Turkish soil. Only in the event of a direct attack would Turkish forces have been committed to a war. Finally, it must be remembered that Turkey invaded northern Cyprus and caused a complete political rearrangement in the island, in total disregard of international norms. This action excited very little response in the West and it looks very much as if Turkey's deed will result in a permanent division of the island. Thus, when it comes to morality, many of the major players in the Gulf crisis are severely flawed and even those in key-supporting roles, such as Cyprus and Israel, are defending what is in terms of UN declarations the indefensible.

While there has been fundamental support among the allied leaders for the actions of the UN-US, feelings among the general Western populace have been very much more divided. There appears to have been least public debate in Great Britain, where polls consistently showed some 60 per cent in favour of war if Iraq refused to leave Kuwait. In contrast, in Italy, less than 20 per cent favoured military intervention (*Time*, 10 December 1990). Even in France, which has maintained a firmly supported line, only 36 per cent of the population favoured involvement in a Gulf war. As was observed in a quotation from *Figaro* (*Time*, 10 December 1990): 'There are so many injustices in the world that it could be useless to be hit hard defending great principles that suddenly appear to belong to another era.'

Legal constraints have spared Germany the necessity to donate troops, but it has pledged some $2.2 billion in support. Thus, Germany has been able to maintain a cautious distance and concern itself more with its own internal problems. Similarly, Japan, the country most dependent upon Gulf oil, has been extremely cautious. With only 19 per cent of the population supporting the dispatch of Self-Defence Force troops outside Japan, the idea was dropped. Indeed, far from regarding the potential for war with horror, many Japanese are reported as seeing the possibilities for economic and diplomatic gain. In the event, the Japanese have pledged a similar figure to the Germans in support of the allied effort.

If world opinion, East and West, Arab and non-Arab, is weighed, there would seem to have been an underlying, but clearly growing consensus for an Arab solution to the crisis. It was realized, particularly in the Arab world, that should Arab be pitted against Arab in any such Western-dominated conflict, the idea of the Arab family would be destroyed for a very long time to come. In the resulting vacuum, the ultimate beneficiaries would be the non-Arab states of Iran and Israel. It was, of course, the elevation of Iran and particularly its fundamentalist doctrine which originally united a large part of the Arab world in the Iraqi cause.

The build-up

Various approaches were adopted in the build-up against Iraq. World opinion, was bombarded with some fine displays of rhetoric, but remained generally unconvinced of the necessity for war. At the same time, substantial pressure was applied through the twin-track approach of the imposition of sanctions and the positioning of an ever-increasing multinational military force along the Kuwait–Saudi Arabian border. From these activities no clear signal emerged. The main reason for this was the mismatch in the 'operational time frames'. It was realized from the outset that sanctions would take years rather than months to be effective, but they would be the preferred option. On any scale, from financial to moral, it would cost far less. If the military were present merely to force sanctions and to prevent any possible Iraqi move into Saudi Arabia, then a force of modest proportions would be required. The fact was that the United States, strongly supported by Great Britain, insisted upon an alternative military option, resulting in a far larger force which could be characterized as offensive rather than defensive. Such was the feeling of public opinion, particularly in the United States, that every belligerent statement from the President or the Secretary of State had to be matched by something calmer and more measured. Thus, one day war appeared inevitable, while on the next a negotiated settlement was the most likely outcome. This set of mixed signals automatically reduced pressure upon Iraq and gave Saddam Hussein virtually a free hand to out-manoeuvre the West politically.

A further point at issue was whether the military assemblage could be truly characterized as a UN force. So strong and forceful had been the US leadership and so predominant were the US military that this question must be raised. Furthermore, the emplacement of the force occurred well before any UN resolution relating to the use of force. While sanctions formed the chief thrust of UN strategy, the requirement was only for a limited, virtually token, military presence. In fact, the military posture changed from passive to potentially offensive, well in advance of the appropriate UN resolution. This change was identified by military experts using as criteria not only the number of troops but, more importantly, the types of weapon being installed.

The confusion over signals was further exacerbated by changes in President Bush's stated objectives. On 8 August in an address to the nation he listed four objectives:

1. Iraq's immediate and unconditional withdrawal from Kuwait;
2. the restoration of Kuwait's legitimate government;
3. the security of the Gulf, including the oilfields; and
4. the safeguarding of US lives.

Each of these, of course, bears further scrutiny. Given that Iraq had at least some genuine grievance against Kuwait, was it reasonable to expect an unconditional withdrawal? A question could certainly be raised as to the legitimacy or otherwise of the Kuwaiti government. It was legitimate in that the ruling family has been in place for a long time, but it was in no obvious way representative of the people of Kuwait. Would the United States be prepared to force the Al-Sabah family on to an unwilling population? A question might also be raised as to whether the presence of so huge an American force actually did enhance the security of the Gulf. From past experience the only guaranteed enhancement would be of regional anti-Americanism. Similar points could have been made about US lives, but with the release of the hostages this objective had already been realized.

Thus, the achievement of these objectives raised a number of problems. The achievement of these objectives subsequently added to the list by the President raised many more:

1. the removal of the present Iraqi regime;
2. the removal of Saddam Hussein;
3. the removal of Iraq's armaments capability (particularly that concerned with chemical and biological weapons); and
4. the removal of Iraq's nuclear potential.

The satisfactory and lasting removal of a regime can surely only be carried out by the people themselves. If a US-sponsored puppet government were to be installed, it would require constant and costly support and would almost certainly never achieve popularity. Such an illegitimate regime would, in the end, fail. It is clear that Saddam Hussein is protected by the most elaborate security arrangements and he is definitely not a Noriega-type figure. Furthermore, Noriega was a former client, having been supported by the CIA in a country which is effectively a US client-state. Therefore, it is unlikely that Saddam Hussein could be assassinated through some external body. Consequently, his removal could be effected only by his own people or as a direct result of the war. The armaments factories are widely spread throughout Iraq and, with the preparation time that was available before the invasion, it must be assumed that there were considerable stockpiles in place. The nuclear potential of Iraq is somewhat conjectural and the stockpile of materials has been regularly inspected by the International Atomic Agency. The latest of the twice-yearly inspections was conducted between 19 and 22 November 1990 and no change in either the amount or purity of the uranium was reported. On the other hand, Israel is known to possess nuclear weapons and a processing plant at Dimona. This knowledge, when it was revealed, produced little reaction in the West, even when the Israeli employee, Vanunu, who revealed it, was kidnapped from the streets of Rome. Furthermore, of all the countries possessing nuclear devices Israel must be considered perhaps the most likely to use them. Therefore, the prevention of nuclear proliferation must be approached by other means. It is certainly not feasible that as each new country obtains nuclear weapons a war can be fermented to destroy the facilities.

In the *Independent on Sunday* (12 August 1990), the entry of the US military into the Gulf was described as 'a bold but dangerous gamble to regain the superpower baton for the US'. In dispatching the troops, the President described the operation as 'wholly defensive' and said that US troops would not initiate hostilities, but were there to defend themselves, if attacked, Saudi

Arabia and other US friends in the Gulf. These noble sentiments were of course eroded as the US force built up and costs soared. The posture changed from defensive to offensive and eventually the 15 January 1991 deadline was fixed. Indeed, after the arrival of the 82nd Airborne Brigade, it was not defensive weaponry which followed, but strike aircraft, combat troops, tanks and armoured personnel carriers. It was apparent therefore that a twin-track policy of sanctions and the threat of attack was to be pursued from almost the beginning of the crisis.

This was the fourth time in eighteen months that President Bush has used US forces in foreign countries. The previous three occasions all involved comparatively small-scale operations in Panama, the Philippines and Liberia. The force in Saudi Arabia was on a completely different scale, far exceeding that sent to Vietnam or Korea. For many people, particularly the Arabs, this would seem to confirm America's obvious desire to obtain and probably retain a position in the Gulf. However, the use of force in the Middle East by the United States has rarely been successful. From the abortive attempt to free the hostages in Iran (1980) to the bombing of the marines' barracks in Beirut (1983), the attack of Iraq on the USS *Stark* (1987), and the accidental shooting down of an Iranian airbus by the USS *Vincennes* (1988), there has been a series of tragedies. The Iran–Contra affair, from which President Bush did not escape unscathed, blighted the last years of the Reagan administration. Thus, over recent years the military experience of the United States in the Middle East gave little ground for confidence.

However, the sheer scale of the military build-up against Iraq, the state-of-the-art technology involved and the fact that, nominally at least, twenty-eight nations were included in the 'coalition', should certainly have been sufficient to secure the outcome. That the volume of men and *matériel* exceeded anything seen since the Second World War undoubtedly imposed great psychological pressure upon Saddam Hussein and the Iraqi people. In that way it may be considered productive. On the other hand, there was a counter-productive aspect. The imposition of such military might in a fragile area of the globe appeared to many, at the very least, excessive. More importantly, the cost of sustaining the men, the equipment and the logistical infrastructure necessary, itself generated a momentum towards war. The question has to be asked as to whether any such massive arms build-up must inevitably lead to war. In the *Guardian* (6 November 1990) this aspect, the so-called 'weapons effect' of Leonard Berkowiz was discussed.

During the latter part of 1990 and the early part of 1991, psychological pressure was heightened by a media blitz against Saddam Hussein. At least some of this was exposed as mere propaganda, but it all appears to have played a part in convincing the British public of the necessity for war. Indeed, throughout the latter part of the build-up, the only country in which opinion polls did not show oscillations among a general decline in support for a military offensive was Great Britain. A further psychological factor was the well-publicized set of medical preparations and the call-up of reservists. In re-examining the pattern of events, it can be seen that from early January 1991, at the latest, the progress towards war had been gathering a momentum of its own.

The response of Saddam Hussein and his key advisers was a series of moves, designed to split the coalition opposing him. Initially, the factor which received greatest attention was the presence of hostages. On the day of the invasion, there were said to be as many as one million foreign nationals in Kuwait, among them 3000 from Britain. There were a further 1000 British citizens in Iraq and some 3500 US citizens, distributed between Iraq and Kuwait. High as these numbers are, they were completely dwarfed by half a million Egyptians, almost half a million people from the Indian sub-continent and some 90,000 Filipinos. Subsequently, almost one million are said to have left the two countries.

On 20 August 1990, Iraq confirmed that the citizens from the West would be held as a human shield and three days later many of them were shown on Iraqi television. There then followed a series of visits by distinguished people, mainly politicians, which resulted in the gradual release of hostages, during the period 30 August until 6 December 1990. On 18 November, it was announced that all hostages would be released over a three-month period from Christmas onwards, but this statement was countermanded on 6 December when the statement was made that all hostages would be released. By the end of December, according to the *Guardian*, there were under 1000 foreigners remaining in Kuwait and about 5500 in Iraq. (Table 6.1). The release of the hostages by Saddam Hussein removed one of the key elements which had excited Western passions against his regime. A second element, seemingly greatly overplayed, was the damage to life and property caused by his soldiers on their entry into Kuwait. Within a week, twenty soldiers, including a colonel, had been publicly hanged for looting and there is strong evidence from Arab sources to indicate that at least from then on little untoward occurred. Having thereby to some extent defused feelings against him, Saddam Hussein proceeded to attempt to build on feelings for his regime. In particular, of course, he raised the issues of Palestine, dubbed by President Bush as 'linkage'. As a result of the Intifada, Western and indeed world emotions had been aroused on behalf of the Palestinians. Given this and the fact that UN Security Council Resolution 242, requiring the withdrawal of Israel from the Occupied Territories, had been outstanding for twenty-three years, there was a good deal of sympathy for his stance. In many publications, the alacrity with which the US-led alliance tried to enforce the twelve Security Council resolutions against Iraq was contrasted unfavourably with the general disregard of the Palestinian claim. The situation was, of course, exacerbated by various actions of the Israeli military, in particular the Temple Mount shootings. It appeared to many that whereas the Israelis were sheltered by the veto of the United States in the Security Council, the Arabs, despite being guardians of the world's most important resource, were usually accorded short shrift.

A further ploy used by Saddam Hussein was to move Palestinians into Kuwait and to campaign for a referendum, should the Al-Sabah family be in a position to return. These moves were reinforced by a call for greater participation in the government of all the Gulf Cooperation Council countries. Ironically, of course, Saddam Hussein could hardly call for democracy since his own regime can only be characterized as totalitarian.

Table 6.1 Foreigners in Kuwait/Iraq, end December 1990

	Kuwait	Iraq
Britain	443*	725†
US	392	383‡
Japan	6	233§
Canada	14	23
Australia	3	2
Germany	2	13
France	24	14
Belgium	1	5
Italy	—	179
Ireland	26	160
Greece	6	3
Netherlands	3	128
Norway	1	8
Spain	1	—
Poland	unknown	450
Bulgaria	unknown	350
Soviet Union	unknown	3000
Switzerland	—	8
Finland	3	9
Denmark	21	15
Romania	unknown	394
Czechoslovakia	—	40
Yugoslavia	unknown	310

Includes *6 detainees, rest in hiding; †342 detainees; ‡88 detainees; §114 detainees.
Source: the *Guardian*

The effect of Saddam's message has, however, been quite startling in that throughout the relevant parts of the Arabian Peninsula there have been moves towards a broadening of the decision-making group and certainly infrastructural and other improvements. Finally, Saddam's more general calls to rally support were made in the name of the Arab nation and Islam. While the appeal to many of the major Arab states failed, at least at the level of the leadership, that to Islam resulted in a major meeting of fundamentalist leaders in Baghdad in early January 1991. Thus, to a degree, Saddam Hussein had fused the Arabs and the Muslims behind his cause. On the other hand, the fact that his action in entering Kuwait was likely to result in Arab fighting Arab and Muslim attacking Muslim was viewed as potentially disastrous in the long term. The build-up period during the autumn and winter of 1990 was thus characterized by the oscillations of both leaders, President Hussein and President Bush. An awful symmetry was presented as each in turn appeared firstly belligerent and then pacific. The result was that any signals which emerged tended to be extremely blurred.

The situation was scarcely helped by the lack of any direct negotiations.

The United States laid the ground rules and operated through a series of intermediaries. The situation further intensified following the adoption of UN Security Council Resolution 678, the ultimatum authorizing the use of 'all necessary means' if Iraq failed to withdraw from Kuwait by 15 January. Despite posturing by both sides, the meeting between the two main actors in the persons of their Foreign Secretaries, Baker and Aziz in Geneva did not occur until 9 January, only six days before the deadline. A further flurry of activity followed, including an abortive attempt by Perez de Cuellar and an even later intervention by the French government. Secret negotiations at various levels had clearly been continuing throughout the later part of the period, but all proved in vain.

Meanwhile, sanctions were having an effect as indicated in *Time* (21 January 1991) and in various interviews conducted by one of the authors (Ewan Anderson) in the region. The inventory as of 15 January, presented in *Time*, read as follows:

1. Iraq will run out of foreign currency reserves by the spring;
2. the embargo has cost Iraq 50 per cent of its GNP;
3. bread, sugar and soap are rationed;
4. imports of industrial goods, raw materials, semi-finished goods and machinery have been reduced by more than 90 per cent;
5. scarcity of tires, spare parts and lubricants is affecting buses, cars and taxis;
6. on average per capita food consumption in Iraq is estimated at 1800 calories a day, down from 3100 before sanctions; and
7. the country's military effectiveness will begin to decline in six to twelve months.

Thus, it appears that by January 1991 sanctions were beginning to cripple Iraq, but, as the article points out, this did not mean that Saddam would necessarily pull out of Kuwait. Nonetheless, the evidence undoubtedly underpins the argument that sanctions should have been given a longer period to operate.

While the time factor was likely to improve the position with regard to sanctions, the effect on the military was likely to be less satisfactory. Although it seemed most unlikely from the start of the action that the Iraqi military would strike first, coalition forces still had to remain on their guard. To be in a state of readiness for anything up to five months demands extremely good discipline, particularly when it is known that the other side is not so constrained. A routine of preparatory exercises interspersed with long periods of boredom is clearly not the best preparation for the eventual hostilities. However, from the point of view of the US government, the greater constraint was probably that of economics. Having, rightly or wrongly, decided to send in such a huge force, the cost of maintaining it, despite heavy subsidies from Arabian Peninsula states, proved prohibitive. For the US troops, rest and recreation facilities were provided, but only on a limited scale. Arab moores effectively prohibited the establishment of facilities such as those in Thailand and the Philippines, which are generally enjoyed by US servicemen overseas. The long-term effects of even meagre provision made were a source of concern to the Arabs.

Viewing the build-up period as a whole, it is difficult to assess the effectiveness of either side. Neither made completely convincing arguments. The reasons for the Iraqi invasion were, in general terms, not accepted, the complete support of the Arab world was not enlisted and the twin-track approach, involving linkage with the Palestinian situation did not, in the end, convince the leadership which counted, that of the United States. On the other hand, the case for moving from sanctions to war was not well made and the reasons for rejecting a full Middle East peace conference were unconvincing. The one success which may, with hindsight, be seen as having been crucial, was the *rapprochement* between Iraq and Iran. From 10 September 1990, when Iraq and Iran agreed to renew full diplomatic relations, Saddam Hussein had no need to guard his very long northern border. Furthermore, freedom of movement in that region presented him with his best opportunity for sanction-breaking. To these obvious dividends was added, during the hostilities, the opportunity to save part of his airforce.

The war option

From 2 August 1990 until 15 January 1991, there was continuous debate over the issue of war. For some, the issue was whether it should be prosecuted at all, for others, only when it should start. Such viewpoints depended upon perceptions of the aims of the exercise and also of the effectiveness of sanctions. It is possible that, some twenty-five years having elapsed since the end of the Vietnam war, feelings of pain and horror had been replaced by ideas of glory. Indeed, it seems very unlikely that only a few years ago any American President could have contemplated such a conflict. The removal of the Soviet threat obviously added a new dimension to the geopolitics of global warfare and left the United States as effectively the sole superpower and 'policeman'. Nonetheless, the change in American sentiments has been marked, although the fissures in society, produced by Vietnam, have not as yet entirely grown over.

Assuming that they had worked, the great advantage of sanctions would have been that they truly heralded a new international order in which the great decisions of mankind were not necessarily taken by resort to armed might. They could also have led to the fall of Saddam Hussein at the hands of his own people. On the other hand, they could have resulted in a partial withdrawal, leaving the regime virtually intact. The maintenance of the coalition, and particularly its Arab component, would probably have presented fewer problems than might have obtained during the hostilities. The other major concomitant of success through sanctions would have been that the West and, in particular, the United States and the United Kingdom would not so easily have been portrayed as hostile to the Arab world.

With the huge array of technically sophisticated armaments available, any doubts as to the outcome of the war, at least in the long term, could scarcely stand reasoned argument. However, short wars are rare and the record of the Iraqi military, admittedly against a fellow Third World opponent, showed that it could be very effective. Thus, it was not the outcome but the time factor required to achieve whatever could be regarded as victory which was in question.

Theoretically, victory in war would have a number of possible advantages. Firstly, Kuwait would be completely liberated and there would be no question of what to do in the event of a partial withdrawal. Secondly, there would be an obvious opportunity not only to destroy the regime, but also its chemical, nuclear and biological potential. Thirdly, there would be an element of retribution, following the alleged atrocities in Kuwait, which, some think, should be exacted. Western oil supplies would be secured and, to maintain the status quo, presumably Western garrisons would be set up at various places in the Gulf region. The most compelling argument against war was that it was open-ended and the ultimate results could not have been foreseen. There was also the crucial question of what happens after hostilities have ceased. If Western or UN forces are emplaced at vital locations, the situation would be controlled for about six months. After that, several regimes would probably topple, to be replaced by those of a definitely anti-Western bias. Furthermore, the cost, financial and measured in other terms, would be enormous and would increase over time. Another key issue was of course the loss of life and injury to the civilian population of Kuwait and Iraq. If this were to continue for any period, condemnation would grow in all corners of the Arab and Muslim worlds. Ideally, the Arabs think of themselves as one nation, the Ummah, and sustained losses in Kuwait and Iraq would not be acceptable. Indeed, the more bloody the war became, the greater support there was likely to be, not only for the Arabs who are in the battle zone, but also for Saddam Hussein himself.

A further factor is environmental damage. There have been many hotly contested assessments of what this might entail. It was argued that should the Kuwaiti and also, possibly, certain Saudi oilfields be bombed and set on fire, air pollution might be a problem. More certain is the fact that water pollution would almost undoubtedly occur.

Western economies would suffer considerably from the loss of a measurable part of the Middle Eastern oil supplies. Therefore, during a war it would seem to be extremely unwise for the coalition to bomb Iraqi or Kuwaiti oilfields. The economies of the states within the region would also suffer, as both Iraq and Kuwait would require a degree of rebuilding. If in fact the desalination plants of Kuwait were put out of action, there would be even more immediate problems.

Other arguments against war included the strength of public opinion, particularly in Europe, and also of the peace movement world-wide. It was thought that there could be large-scale violence, particularly in Muslim countries. Added to this was the potential for terrorism, threatened in detail by Saddam Hussein. It was reported that a meeting of 150 key terrorist leaders took place in Baghdad in early January 1991, but this may well be merely propaganda. As security throughout the Western World would probably be particularly strict during any period of hostilities, the potential for terrorist activity would of course be greatly reduced.

Finally, such a huge military presence as that of the US and its supporters required a vast logistical infrastructure. Whether resupply from industry in anything other than a very short war would be sufficient must be doubtful. Indeed, should the war have continued for a period of months, both the United States and the United Kingdom could have suffered from an embarrassing shortage of *matériel*.

The just war

Many of the finest minds produced by Christianity, from St Augustine through St Thomas Aquinas to the present day, have been exercised on the question of a just war. That Christianity and war have long been associated is obvious. Christian orders such as the Knights of St John of Jerusalem became effectively armies in the defence of Christendom. Various criteria against which potential hostilities can be judged have been advanced, but these still leave ample room for discussion and disagreement. On the other hand, there would seem to be general accord on the issue of the major nuclear weapons. There cannot be justice in the utter destruction of God's creation.

With regard to the Gulf crisis, there have been comparatively heated exchanges through articles and letters in most of the major newspapers. Opponents of war on the grounds of justice have included most notably the Bishop of Sodor and Man and the Principal of Salisbury and Wells Theological College. The most vociferous spokesman to support the justice of war against Iraq has been the Bishop of Oxford. No attempt can be made to summarize points made during the centuries of thinking on the concept of the just war, but there are four key pointers. In very basic terms, a war may be considered just if there is justice in the cause, the authority, the means and the hope for outcome. War should only be entered when all other avenues have been exhausted, but, it has been expressed by many, that evil thrives when good people do nothing.

In the case under discussion the cause was the occupation of Kuwait, but there were many other motives, particularly that of the conservation of oil supplies. Authority was derived from Security Council Article No. 42 and the means, restricted to conventional weapons, might be considered just. However, there must be some concern over the vast discrepancy in levels of technology between the two sides. Most controversy has centred on the question of the outcome. If a war were to be fought over the specifically local area of Kuwait and was restricted basically to Kuwait, then there might be some case for justice. If, however, Iraq were devastated and the Arab world was as a result left with little protection against either Iran or Israel, it would be difficult to define the outcome as peace with justice. Unlike the Falklands war, which was clearly constrained by the geography of the situation, a war at the head of the Gulf could lead to a regional or even global conflagration. Therefore, as there must be such doubts about the aftermath of a war, the concept of a potentially just war, in this context, must be judged 'not proved'.

The war itself

During the period immediately before the war there was intense speculation about all possible aspects of the outcome. With such a slow and measured build-up no previous war had been analysed in advance to such a degree. Prewar reasoning followed the lines indicated below.

In a war, given the allied military supremacy, the basic aim of the Iraqi military would be to capitalize upon the fact that they were only interested in defence. It was known that they had constructed elaborate fortifications around Kuwait and had laid minefields on the land and at sea. With those, together with the sheer numbers of their personnel and tanks, they posed a formidable opposition. The other key factor in their favour was the highly trained Republican Guard which would provide reinforcements when required. From this solid base, which many experts considered would be sufficient to ensure a prolonged encounter, a number of other approaches could be considered. There could have been an Iraqi first strike, but psychologically this would probably have been counter-productive. If Saddam Hussein were to stand as protector of the Arab world, he could do so more effectively after he had been attacked. On the other hand, a first strike in the land battle would be a greater possibility. Immediately prior to the onslaught, the allied forces would be exposed and such a strike could be devastating for morale.

Iraq was assumed to possess large stockpiles of chemical and biological weapons and these posed both a psychological and a physical threat. Both, of course, might misfire and affect the Iraqi troops and both would be received with world-wide condemnation. Judging by the use of chemical weapons during the war with Iran, they were most likely to be used in desperation. Since Iraq would be concerned to conserve all *matériel*, a chemical or biological onslaught would probably be saved until temperatures were somewhat higher during late spring or early summer. To combat such an attack, protective clothing would need to be worn and this would severely constrain the effectiveness of the allied troops. The result of even one such attack would be significant in that precautions would have to be taken during every subsequent attack, even if all proved to be conventional only.

Apart from direct attacks upon the allied positions, the Iraqi leadership also attempted to enlarge the scope of the war by drawing in other countries. The most obvious way of doing this was through attacks on Israel. However, unless they were reasonably severe, Israel might be prevailed upon not to respond, since such restraint would be likely to secure a reward at a subsequent Middle East peace conference. Certainly, should Israel enter the war, it would be difficult to see that Arab troops could fight on the same side.

Being the offensive side, the allied forces would be expected largely to dictate the character of the war. Assuming sanctions and diplomacy without the actual use of force had been ruled out, the simplest and possibly the most effective offensive act might have been the assassination of Saddam Hussein. However, with his tightly organized personal security structure, it is very doubtful whether this could have been achieved other than by an Iraqi in the inner circle. In other parts of the Middle East, Mossad has been known to have infiltrated to that kind of level, but evidence available seemed to show that in the case of Iraq this was unlikely. The CIA is precluded by Presidential decree from such activity, but even if a blind eye were turned in this case, the problems involved would seem to be too extreme.

In the event of armed conflict, strategists were generally agreed that there would be three overall approaches to a war against Iraq. A frontal assault would entail the use of allied technical superiority to break Iraqi defences under a massive onslaught. In this scenario, Kuwait would either be taken directly, or cut off from supplies and there would be a thrust deep into Iraq, probably as far as Baghdad. A more subtle approach, favoured by others, among them Henry Kissinger, could be designated 'surgical'. This would involve the gradual removal of Iraqi economic and military assets by air strikes (Figure 6.1). Refineries, factories, airfields, communications buildings and military concentrations would come under sustained attack in the hope that Iraqi morale would fail. Should this not be the case, the war machine would still be sufficiently weakened that an allied land attack would achieve success comparatively rapidly. The third scenario took into account the strength of the Iraqi pre-positioning and would be diversionary. Attacks would be made along the Saudi Arabian–Iraqi border in an attempt to lure the Republican Guard out of position and to engage it directly. This would leave other allied forces with the opportunity to cut off Kuwait from its supply lines. In all three cases, the land battle would be preceded by a prolonged air assault to gain air supremacy and to damage the Iraqi army.

The possible course of events was encapsulated by The Guardian (14 January 1991) in three scenarios. 'The Pentagon's dream scenario' consisted of a six-day war, fought almost entirely in the air. After the establishment of air superiority in two days, the major military defences and strategic installations of Iraq would have been removed by day four and on day five Saddam Hussein would sue for peace and withdraw from Kuwait, leaving the allied forces to advance unopposed.

The 'textbook' scenario required four weeks of air, ground and naval operations. After day four, air superiority would have been established and after day ten, the major military Iraqi assets would have been reduced by massive bombing. The remaining seventeen days would consist of an air, land and sea offensive, including outflanking tank manoeuvres to draw off the Republican Guards and an amphibious assault along the coastline around Kuwait city itself.

At the other extreme, the 'nightmare' scenario was dictated from Baghdad, Tel Aviv and Paris, rather than Washington. Air strikes were only partially effective and much of the Iraqi infrastructure remained undamaged. As a result of missile attacks, Israel became embroiled in the conflict, producing a division in Arab loyalties. Kuwaiti oil installations were destroyed and US troops suffered heavy losses. Iranian intervention occurred and France, capitalizing on Arab divisions, emerged to take credit for the eventual liberation of a war-torn Kuwait.

With twenty-eight nations, including the one world superpower, ranged

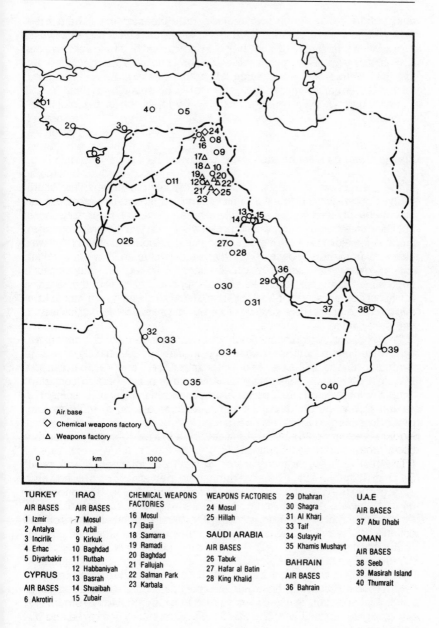

TURKEY	IRAQ	CHEMICAL WEAPONS	WEAPONS FACTORIES	29 Dhahran	U.A.E
AIR BASES	AIR BASES	FACTORIES	24 Mosul	30 Shagra	AIR BASES
1 Izmir	7 Mosul	16 Mosul	25 Hillah	31 Al Kharj	37 Abu Dhabi
2 Antalya	8 Arbil	17 Baiji		33 Taif	
3 Incirlik	9 Kirkuk	18 Samarra	SAUDI ARABIA	34 Sulayyit	OMAN
4 Erhac	10 Baghdad	19 Ramadi	AIR BASES	35 Khamis Mushayt	AIR BASES
5 Diyarbakir	11 Rutbah	20 Baghdad	26 Tabuk		38 Seeb
	12 Habbaniyah	21 Fallujah	27 Hafar al Batin	BAHRAIN	39 Masirah Island
CYPRUS	13 Basrah	22 Salman Park	28 King Khalid	AIR BASES	40 Thumrait
AIR BASES	14 Shuaibah	23 Karbala		36 Bahrain	
6 Akrotiri	15 Zubair				

Figure 6.1 Key air bases and weapons factories

against Iraq, the 'textbook' scenario appeared the most likely of the three. However, it was realized that Saddam Hussein would have had a very long preparation time for the conflict and, despite 'carpet' bombing and 'surgical' strikes, his major assets would at least, in part, survive. Therefore, while the eventual course of the war might follow that envisaged in the 'textbook' scenario, the time required would probably be significantly longer. The longer the conflict, the greater must be the likelihood of the 'nightmare scenario'.

Effects of war on neighbouring states

In the event of war it was considered that the key player would be Israel. With its previous experience in such encounters, the Israeli air force would be capable of effective 'surgical' strikes in Iraq. However, the entry of Israel into the conflict would have posed problems for all Arab and Muslim states. Since the major issue during the negotiating period was 'linkage', it was essential, from the allied viewpoint, that Israel continued its policy of taking only a low-profile interest in proceedings. However, this might prove impossible, given the strong Palestinian support for Iraq. In the event, it might not be necessary for Iraq to carry out strikes in Israel, as it was thought that the Palestinians themselves might open up several fronts, particularly on the West Bank.

The other highly significant neighbour would be Iran, which appeared to be involved in sanction-breaking. On the one hand, Iran would like to remain neutral so that it could be seen as an untarnished force at the post-war Middle East peace conference. On the other hand, Iran shares Iraq's antipathy for Western and, particularly, American activity in the Gulf. The natural inclination of Iranian fundamentalists would be to offer support, probably covert, to Iraq.

Jordan, economically by far the weakest of the neighbouring states, has been heavily dependent upon Iraq and transit trade from Aqaba. Furthermore, the population seemed to be overwhelmingly in support of Saddam Hussein. King Hussein, during the period from 2 August 1990, emerged as the one world-standard diplomat in the region. He made every effort to initiate an Arab settlement of the dispute, but even his subtle diplomacy might, in the end, result in the demise of his dynasty and his country. Since it is at the mercy of its more powerful neighbours, Jordan could afford to side wholly with Iraq, but if it appeared to waver over-much, it might suffer at the hands of Iraq.

The case of Yemen was far more clear-cut in that it would like to secure the return of Asir Province. This would only occur after the partial break-up of Saudi Arabia, which itself could only result from an inconclusive outcome to the crisis and, probably, the replacement of the ruling family. Yemen has already lodged a boundary claim against Saudi Arabia and it consistently supported Iraq throughout the crisis.

It was considered that Saudi Arabia, along with all the smaller Gulf states, would become considerably less stable in the event of a prolonged war.

Having already been the objects of Saddam Hussein's wrath as a result of their vast wealth and its unequal distribution, they would be likely to see at least major internal political changes.

Were the present Iraqi regime not destroyed in a war, Syria would find itself in an extremely difficult position. The rivalry between the two Ba'athist regimes and, in particular, between their two leaders, has already resulted in a climate of extreme animosity. Should Saddam Hussein be in any position to launch further initiatives, the major target would certainly be Syria. Mindful of this, it seems likely that Syrian support for any allied offensive would be a good deal less than wholehearted and some covert support might well be offered to Iraq. However, Syria has much to lose, given its new-found standing with the West. Diplomatic relations with both the United States and the United Kingdom have been restored and military activity in Lebanon, although in many ways similar to that of Iraq in Kuwait, appears not to have been queried.

With the fifth largest army in the world, membership of NATO and the support of the United States, Turkey had far less to fear directly, in the event of war, than any other neighbouring country. Troops had already been moved to the frontier with Iraq and the accent had been on defence. However, the potential importance of the Turkish NATO air bases meant that there would be strong pressure for Turkey to take an increasingly anti-Iraqi stance. Indeed, it was thought that were it to do so, the gains could be very significant. With the demise of Saddam Hussein's regime, Turkey might even gain some territory at the expense of Iraq. More likely, however, would be its insistence on the establishment of an autonomous Kurdish state in northern Iraq. This would provide a focus for Kurdish sentiment and reduce internal Kurdish pressure in Turkey. Furthermore, having supported the UN–US approach, Turkey could find itself the most important power in the Middle East. On the other hand, should Saddam survive, relations would be strained for a very long time and Turkey's hopes of cooperative development within the Tigris–Euphrates Basin would be dashed.

It is safe to assume that all the neighbouring states were aware of the variety of possible outcomes to any conflict. Therefore, their overt and covert dealings might well have been diametrically opposed. The least equivocal seems to have been Egypt, almost certainly as a result of the major inputs of US aid it receives. Since the Camp David Accords, the United States has, in the context of aid, tended to treat Israel and Egypt in an even-handed fashion, with the result that Egyptian stability is very much dependent upon such aid. However, there are significant fundamentalist concentrations in Egypt and in a conflict the Suez Canal would be a vital artery for allied resupply. Should there be a long conflict and, particularly, should Israel join in, it was reasoned that the future of the Mubarak regime would look distinctly doubtful.

The great imponderable, nevertheless, remained the Soviet Union. Throughout the period of the crisis, the Soviets backed the US line, despite their former high level of support for Iraq. This approach was adopted presumably to safeguard the newly fashioned US–Soviet détente and, more immediately, to ensure the flow of Western aid for its crippled economy.

However, should events in the Baltic States represent the first stage in a military coup, the position might change radically. Soviet advisers and technicians remained in Iraq during the war, the number reported varying from 3000 to 150, but their role could only be surmised. Were they to be revealed as vital assets for the Iraqi military, the neutrality of the Soviet Union would be, in a measure, compromised. As things stand, in the post-war period the Soviet Union, having avoided any military involvement, would be likely to benefit greatly economically and politically. Arab feelings towards the Soviets would be expected to contrast sharply with the generally anti-American and anti-British sentiment.

The post-war period

Speculation about post-war events, since they would be so highly dependent upon the actual outcome of the war, could only be the subject of conjecture. The sole possible results would seem to be an allied victory or a stalemate, with the former by far the more likely. However, the effects in the region would also be tempered by such factors as the length of the conflict, the character of the war and the identity of the participants. A short, sharp victory would result in comparative stability, whereas a long-drawn-out and bloody conflict could lead to major changes. In the extreme case of the conflict overspilling widely from the region it seemed possible that the global geopolitical balance itself might be affected. The one certainty would seem to be that UN or US forces would be required for a comparatively long period to police the region. In that case, the fragmentation of Iraq or Saudi Arabia, posited by a number of commentators, seemed unlikely. A power balance within the region requires a strong Iraq as the Arab bastion against adventurism from Israel or Iran. Saudi Arabia, having hosted and provided financial support for the allied build-up, would expect help in combating any centrifugal forces. Nevertheless, in the longer term, with the departure of the peace-keeping units, the requirement of the populations throughout the Gulf Cooperation Council states for greater participation seems likely to lead to a change in the character of the regimes. Furthermore, if, as is currently conceived, the peace-keeping duties were carried out by predominantly US forces, the question must arise as to how long they could be maintained in the region. Five months for an admittedly larger force has imposed a great strain upon the US economy already and, without more obvious support from other First World countries, the United States might be tempted to make an early departure.

The question of reparations by Iraq for damage in Kuwait and, possibly, other neighbouring countries, is hardly a realistic idea. Before the war, Iraq was already one of the highest indebted countries in the world and, following the destruction of much of its industry during the conflict, the position is far worse. The emphasis must surely be on rehabilitating Iraq as an Arab force, rather than on extracting vengeance. The possibility of bringing the leadership and, particularly Saddam Hussein himself to trial for war crimes would also pose many problems. Apart from the fact that many of his crimes were perpetrated with the connivance of the West, such trials could only be effectively conducted under the auspices of the United Nations. As yet, the UN has no facilities constituted for war crimes trials.

Speculation, but now only speculation, about a stalemate, as effectively occurred in Vietnam and the Iran–Iraq war, envisaged the 'nightmare' scenario. With the same regime in place and a reasonably strong military intact, Iraq would have continued to pose a threat to particularly the Gulf states, Syria and Israel. Thus, a far larger 'police' force would have been required and this would have been extremely difficult to sustain. The status of Saddam Hussein himself would have been greatly enhanced and, in the Arab world, he would have been seen as a direct descendant of Saladin and Nasser. More importantly, Iraq would have been a strong voice in any subsequent Middle East peace conference. However, despite the various strategic problems which faced the allied forces, this outcome was always considered extremely unlikely.

In fact, the war followed broadly along the lines of the text book scenario except that the emphasis on the aeriel bombardment was far greater than envisaged. Against the most savage and sustained onslaught ever mounted, Iraq, essentially still a developing country, crumbled.

Notes

1. Abu-Hakima-Ahmad Mustafa, *The Modern History of Kuwait, 1750–1965*, p. 1, Luzac, London, 1983.
2. Abu-Hakima-Ahmad Mustafa, *The Modern History of Kuwait, 1750–1965*, op. cit. p. 147, Luzac, 1983.
3. Dickson, H.R.P., *Kuwait and Her Neighbours*, p. 274, George Allen and Unwin Ltd., London, 1956.
4. ibid.
5. Mezerik, A.G. *Kuwait–Iraq Dispute, 1961*, p. 6, International Review Service, New York, USA, 1961.
6. Cordesman, H. Anthony, *The Gulf and the Search for Strategic Stability*, p. 403, Westview Press, London, 1984.
7. Schofield, R.N. and Blake, G.H. (eds), *Arabian Boundaries, 1853–1957*, Vol. 2, Archive Editions, London, 1988.
8. ibid.
8. Times Books, New York, 1990.

Chapter 7
The view from the region

One of the authors, Ewan Anderson, spent a large part of the period from early November 1990 until 12 January 1991 collecting views on the crisis within the region. He visited a Mediterranean country, Malta, a part-Mediterranean, part-Middle Eastern country, Turkey and a Middle Eastern country, the United Arab Emirates. In each, he was able to discuss the range of problems with government officials, academics and journalists and to obtain some feel for the prevailing view. He was also able to monitor newspaper, radio and television coverage. The views from the two regions represent, of course, those held before the onset of hostilities.

The Mediterranean viewpoint was summarized by Professor Guido de Marco, a Maltese, who, speaking as President of the UN General Assembly, linked a Gulf war to possible conflict in Israel and thence the Mediterranean Basin. Israel is seen as the key to future Mediterranean involvement in the Gulf crisis, since a conflagration there would include Syria and possibly Egypt as well. In the end, it might result in a US, UN or NATO confrontation with the Arab world.

The second major player was thought to be Turkey, a NATO country with deep Middle Eastern involvement. With such initiatives as the Grand Anatolian Project, involving both the Tigris and the Euphrates, and the 'Peace Pipeline', Turkey is closely linked politically and economically with its Arab neighbours to the east. Indeed, according to President Ozal, with whom Ewan Anderson spoke, Turkey is particularly anxious to develop close ties, based upon mutual dependence for water, oil and food, with not only Iraq but also the countries of the Gulf Cooperation Council. Thus, in the event of hostilities, Turkey could find itself in an extremely difficult situation. Two particularly compelling views from discussions in Turkey indicated that sanctions appeared to be working, although Iran was probably offering covert assistance to Iraq, and that any land attack on Iraq would lead to a general Arab uprising. Turkey aimed, as far as possible, to remain neutral.

If a conflict should spread to the Mediterranean, the position could well be exacerbated by Arab nationalism, fundamentalism and terrorism. Despite the great differences between the Arab countries in population, wealth and political outlook, there remains a strong feeling for the Arab nation. The idea was most effectively encouraged by President Nasser and, subsequently, the only individual to achieve anything approaching the same status has been Saddam Hussein. Despite his obviously flawed character, he does confront the West and First World manipulation of the Third World. This is particularly appreciated in the Mediterranean Basin, which itself effectively divides the First World from the Third World.

Since the election of a fundamentalist government in Algeria, the idea of fundamentalism, whether Sunni or Shiite, does not appear quite so fanciful as it once did. While the idea of a conflict between Christendom and Islam, setting the Gulf region and the Mediterranean ablaze, seems somewhat extreme, it is viewed as the ultimate possibility. If a war should spread into the Mediterranean Basin, NATO would be involved and a further increase in participants would become almost inevitable.

The Mediterranean is not only the cradle of civilization, but also of terrorism. In the twenty-year period from 1970, over one-third of all terrorist incidents have occurred within the region. Israel and all the states along the northern shore have been involved. Furthermore, Mediterranean states have been implicated in government deals with terrorists, in terrorist training and in terrorism itself. The possibilities for terrorism are heightened by the profusion of targets, ranging from water and oil pipelines to the shipping concentrations in key straits, such as those between the Black Sea and the Mediterranean, Suez and Gibraltar. Since world-wide terrorism has been threatened by Saddam Hussein, there are genuine worries about the activities of such organizations as Abu Nidal and Hezbollah in such a volatile region.

Additionally, it is realized that three nuclear powers — the Soviet Union, France and Israel — have access to the Mediterranean and the construction of an 'Islamic Bomb' is always a possibility. Further, nine states within the Mediterranean Basin possess chemical weapons, the greatest concentration of such an arsenal in the world. Thus, the possibility of any overspill from a Gulf conflict into the Mediterranean is viewed with grave disquiet.

Within the Gulf, the predominant view among Arabs is that the United States was desperate to get back into the region, to control the key world resource, oil. With the potential development of Europe, following EC 1992, there was a real danger that the United States might be sidelined on the world stage, but by its rapid thrust into the region and massive military build-up, it has assured itself of a central role. The interpretation of Saddam Hussein's meeting with April Glaspie is therefore that the United States was not at all worried about Saddam's actions. Furthermore, they see collusion with Saudi Arabia, which was viewing the various minor democratic experiments in Kuwait with obvious distaste. Therefore, the crisis is seen as a mere continuation of history in which the great powers have in turn exercised their influence in the Gulf region.

Another strongly held view is that the Arabs and Israel have always been treated differently. UN Security Council Resolution 242 has been outstanding since 1967 and, if anything, Israeli adventurism has been encouraged. Thus, although the invasion of Kuwait may have had nothing whatever to do with the Palestinian cause, linkage is still seen as vital.

While Saddam Hussein himself is generally not at all popular, he is seen as the one man who has stood up to the West and Israel. It is seen as his mistake that he did not perhaps occupy Kuwait for one week and then withdraw. In that event, he would have shown his distaste for the GCC regimes, but would also have eschewed the type of violence condemned when perpetrated by Israel. However, most Arabs assert the necessity to separate Saddam Hussein and his regime, which they see as evil, and the Iraqi people. For the Arabs a strong Iraq is critical if their voice, particularly in the Palestinian conflict, is ever to be heard. Indeed, they would go further and suggest that if there is to be any regional power balance, a strong Iraq is vital. Therefore, it is not in the interests of the United States to destroy the Iraqi military. Since in this both Arab and Western views seem to coincide, they conclude that a war is unlikely. Both sides have too much to lose.

As in the Mediterranean, in the Gulf Turkey was considered to be a key actor in the crisis. By behaving as a buffer or even playing an active role, Turkey might be in a position to speed up the success of its application to join the European Community. Furthermore, as a powerful country in its own right, and with the support of NATO, Turkey has a greater freedom of action than any other country in the region.

The land war launched against Iraq on 23/24 February 1991 was perceived to have a successful outcome. It did not result in the predicted withdrawal of support for UN forces from Egypt and Syria. However, there was support for Iraq amongst the large concentration of fundamentalists in Egypt, and in any future conflict their role could be critical.

Many Arabs had considered a war unlikely as it could be open–ended. Indeed, the war may now be over but the region certainly does not have peace and stability. It had been hoped that European governments would exercise a calming influence on the more belligerent elements in the United States. In fact, some Arabs were horrified at the minor role of the European governments in the various diplomatic endeavours. The failure of these endeavours also suggests that neither leader, President Bush nor Saddam Hussein, wanted to avoid war. There was certainly an unwillingness on either side to lose face. Other crucial factors were the marked US opposition to linkage and the burden imposed by the cost of the US military presence.

As predicted, the post-war period is proving extremely difficult. The UN or US presence may have to be maintained for a long time, unless the US grows weary and decides to withdraw all its forces. Whatever arrangements are made, however, the likelihood is that even if Saddam Hussein is deposed, a series of similar demagogues will inevitably arise, unless the West learns to treat the Arabs in an even-handed fashion and to enter into a continuing dialogue with them.

Chapter 8
Postscript: the war

Arab and many other commentators were wrong. No last-minute Arab peace initiatives were forthcoming and France, the most likely European state, failed in its efforts in negotiations.

Why? Saddam Hussein, as depicted in the Western press, appeared intransigent and unwilling to consider withdrawal from Kuwait. However, it must be stressed that the United States never offered any true negotiations. It was emphasized from the start by the United States that Iraq must gain nothing from its occupation of Kuwait. Since, undoubtedly, there was some provocation and Iraq has genuine grievances over its border with Kuwait, this seems, with hindsight, to have been a particularly harsh judgement. It is a general rule of diplomacy that some sort of ladder, however flimsy, must be offered if there is to be any chance of success. In particular, the question of any linkage with the issue of Palestine was resisted, despite the fact that there are, undeniably, certain similarities.

Perhaps war was the only possibility for Saddam Hussein. Having subjected his people to an eight-year struggle with Iran and having given away the meagre gains, he could hardly withdraw from Kuwait empty-handed. Furthermore, his economy, already devastated after the conflict with Iran, would be in a worse state after sanctions, Iraq would still be a major debtor nation, and Saddam would still have a huge military force which could not be accommodated in a civilian economy.

George Bush, having already used US troops twice during the opening period of his presidency, appeared intent from the start on disabusing those who considered him to be a 'wimp'. There is in fact strong evidence from within the Executive Offices that it was he, personally, rather than the military industrial complex, who provided the impetus towards war. Thus, it may be, despite the reasons made public which in any case varied in priority from speech to speech, that the President felt that he needed to take decisive action to remove Saddam Hussein.

Depending on the viewpoint of the observer, the onset of the war can be attributed to a number of factors. It may be, essentially, a 'High Noon' shoot-out between the leaders, neither of whom would give ground. It is undoubtedly over the control of the world's major resource, oil, and Western influence in the region. The sensitivities of Israel have also played a part in that it is clear that the United States would prefer conflict to linkage. There was also the question of the cost of maintaining and supplying such a vast military force. The actual date was probably influenced by climatic factors, in that any land campaign needs to be complete before the onset of hot weather. At that time, not only would the supply of sufficient potable water cause difficulties, but the wearing of protective suits, inside armoured vehicles, would certainly result in some in heat exhaustion.

Despite the weight of logical argument against it, the conflict which threatened to become a conflagration began on the night of 17/18 January. The media blackout, together with the flow of propaganda from both sides, meant that even after some 20 days, results were difficult to assess. The campaign began, as predicted, with a massive aerial bombardment, far in excess of anything ever seen before. Indeed, the weight of explosives dropped on the first day, alone, matched the power of the atomic bomb which devastated Hiroshima. Well over 2000 sorties were flown each day, the figure peaking at 2900. This can be placed in context when it is realized that the maximum number of sorties ever flown during one week in Vietnam was 3400. The aerial assault, directed initially at Baghdad, Basra, a wide range of military targets, armaments factories and the infrastructure of Iraq, comprised high level 'carpet bombing' by B52s and low level 'precision bombing' by fighter-bombers. In addition, a variety of missiles, including Cruise missiles, were dispatched from aircraft, helicopters and ships. Well before the end of the air bombardment phase, more ordnance had been expended in Iraq and Kuwait, than had been used by all the belligerents throughout the Second World War. After the first two or three days, the attack was entirely unopposed by the Iraqi air force and a little later, opposition from the ground virtually ceased also. Meanwhile, as the attack gathered momentum, B52s were flown from as far away as Diego Garcia, Spain and the United Kingdom.

That the one world superpower, aided by two other First World countries, had unleashed by far the greatest aerial bombardment ever seen, against a Third World country, rather less than the size of Texas, was interpreted in various ways. For the United States military, still scarred by events in Vietnam, it appeared to be a prudent way of ensuring that there could only be one result. To much of the Arab world, the sheer devastation wrought indicated that the liberation of Kuwait was only a minor aim. Certainly, it could be said that the level of destruction in Iraq exceeded anything required to guard against resupply to the Iraqi military in Kuwait. A question was also raised about the identification of targets and the level of precision of much of the bombing. When it was revealed on 14 February that some 400 civilians had been killed in an air-raid shelter, no obvious expressions of regret were forthcoming from either the United States or the United Kingdom military. Indeed, many attempts were made to prove that despite denials by Western reporters on the ground, the target was military. The total death toll of Iraqi civilians will probably never be known, but figures ranging from 50,000 to 100,000 have been advanced.

During the 37 days of the air war, there was virtually saturation media coverage in Western countries. Despite the fog of propaganda, one fact to emerge was that the military were making great efforts to limit the attack to military targets. However, when these included elements of the infrastructure, such as bridges, there was bound to be a high civilian death toll. Undoubtedly, the level of precision was helped by the use of 'smart' weapons, although even these could not be guaranteed. The other main aspect of the coverage which many found disturbing was the unopposed use of high technology against predominantly Third World buildings. Many found the level of 'overkill' obscene, but there is an argument which would justify it in terms of saving Western military lives.

Although with their hardened shelters and decoys, the Iraqis showed that they had used the long preparation period well, their losses were undoubtedly severe and were consistently underestimated by Western media. Furthermore, in the media battle which parallelled the air war, Saddam Hussein had several successes and the original aims of the Allies became submerged in rhetoric. Thus, it was indicated by the United States that, rather than the liberation of Kuwait, the central aim was the destruction of Saddam Hussein's regime. This, of course, went far beyond any Security Council resolutions.

However, despite some successes in his propaganda, Saddam Hussein was unable to prize the Coalition apart. Despite the use of Scud missiles against Israel, the Israeli military did not enter the war. Furthermore, although there were demonstrations throughout the Muslim world in favour of Iraq, no other country offered military support. Curfews were imposed in Egypt and Syria and strong anti-Western feelings were expressed in Iran, but any potential uprisings were controlled and even the Palestinians were constrained from entering the war. As a reward for resisting the urge to enter the fray, Israel received increasingly favourable publicity and should, presumably, expect some reward at any subsequent Middle Eastern Peace Conference.

In the war itself, the only success for Iraq was the capture of a Saudi village, Khafji. This was held for some 24 hours and was celebrated as a triumph. In the end, it proved to be almost the sole example of an Iraqi offensive.

As reported in the media, world-wide peace movements appeared to have little impact upon proceedings. However, during what proved to be the last few days of the air offensive, serious efforts were made to stop the war. Iraq had used at least two sets of proposals, which involved unconditional withdrawal from Kuwait, but, despite having the imprimatur of the Soviet Union, these proved unacceptable to the United States and the United Kingdom. During this period, it became increasingly clear that, although the war was being prosecuted in the name of the United Nations, decision-making was entirely within the hands of President Bush. Despite calls from many quarters for a temporary cessation of hostilities to allow negotiations, the bombing offensive continued and, indeed, increased, focusing upon the potential battle areas in Kuwait and the Kuwait–Iraqi borderland. For many, this proved that President Bush had never been interested in peace, from almost the beginning of the crisis. Further evidence was provided in an article by Cockburn[1], in which three peace initiatives, made during August

1990, alone, are described. For other observers, Saddam Hussein had prevaricated long enough and any lull in fighting would only allow him to reinforce his position.

The land war began on the night of 23/24 February, with a massive movement of tanks and armour into Kuwait and southern Iraq. Resistance was minimal and very soon Kuwait was virtually cut off. The Allied attack was both decisive and devastating and was supported by an aerial assault by fighter-bombers and helicopters. The expected amphibious landing never occurred, despite intensive preparatory minesweeping operations. On the Iraqi side, there were pockets of heavy resistance, but there was no co-ordinated defence. Furthermore, the long awaited assault by the Republican Guard never really materialized. The viciousness of the Western attack was justified in terms of saving Allied lives, terminating atrocities in Kuwait and constraining Iraqi use of chemical and biological weapons. In the event, it transpired that Iraq did not have the capability of projecting such weapons, other than crudely, through drums dropped from aircraft. That this was already known to the military authorities has subsequently emerged and, in view of other examples of disinformation, there must remain some doubts about the scale of atrocities perpetrated by the Iraqis.

After seven days of the land war, half of which were spent in Allied attacks upon retreating Iraqis, a cease-fire was declared on 2 March. Thus, the land war lasted for only some seven days and this defied many earlier predictions. The major reason was probably the loss of morale in the Iraqi military, resulting from a lack of basic provisions. The television picture of an Iraqi conscript, kissing the boot of an American soldier, who was offering refreshment, provided a stark indication of the effectiveness of the Allied bombing on resupply routes, but also offered a potent symbol for future generations of Arabs.

It remains difficult to judge whether this could be accounted a 'just war', in the Augustinian sense, partly, at least, as a result of the successful use of propaganda by both sides. Further historians will reveal something nearer the truth, but it is already clear that the greater part of the oil slick was caused by Allied bombing, that Saddam Hussein had no nuclear and very restricted chemical warfare capability, that the danger posed by the Republican Guard was greatly exaggerated and that the quality of the Iraqi equipment was overstated. On the Iraqi side, the strength of the Allied forces appears to have been completely misjudged and the capability of the Iraqi military, greatly overestimated. Even should Saddam Hussein's major aim have been to withstand hostilities for as long as possible, until the inevitable defeat, he could not, surely, have countenanced the utter devastation of his country which has resulted. Whether he himself survives must be highly conjectural and there must be some concern over the continuing integrity of Iraq itself. Although, in the end, the Arab cause would surely suffer, several countries would stand to gain from its dismemberment. Already, the Iranians and the Saudis have begun vying with each other in their support for the Shiites of the Basra region.

What of the peace? The removal of Saddam Hussein and even his discomfiture by the continuation of sanctions would seem to exceed Security

Council resolutions. Although the continuing United States presence in the region would facilitate the development of a credible opposition in Iraq, it would almost certainly also increase the risk of terrorism. At some stage despite its almost total lack of control over events, the United Nations must be expected to act. Whether what has essentially been a United States action has, in the long term, strengthened or weakened the United Nations, remains to be seen. Israel, Egypt, Turkey and Saudi Arabia have all provided strong support and can expect to be rewarded by the West. In at least one plan, already revealed, they would form the poles in a multi-polar Middle Eastern development structure. Syria and Iran also provided support, but, given their immediate past, their future, as viewed by the West, must be less clear. The Kurdish people may gain something, possibly an autonomous region within Iraq, but the Palestinians, the PLO and Jordan, through their support for Iraq, have undoubtedly lost standing. Having denied 'linkage' to Saddam Hussein, will the Western powers now seek it on their own behalf? Will Security Council Resolution 242, outstanding for almost 24 years, be finally addressed?

With so many problems outstanding and an increasing desire for participation, if not democracy itself, throughout the region, the only certain conclusion seems to be that in the Middle East, stability will remain elusive. The likelihood must remain that the Gulf War of 1991 will, in time, be seen as merely one more episode in the long history of conflict within the region.

Note

1. Cockburn, A., 'In for the Kill', *New Statesman and Society*, 22 February 1991.

Index